APPLESEEDS

* ❋ *

A TEN-WEEK
NURTURING PROGRAM
FOR PRETEEN GIRLS

Betty Huizenga

David C Cook®

transforming lives together

APPLESEEDS
Published by David C. Cook
4050 Lee Vance View
Colorado Springs, CO 80918 U.S.A.

David C. Cook Distribution Canada
55 Woodslee Avenue, Paris, Ontario, Canada N3L 3E5

David C. Cook U.K., Kingsway Communications
Eastbourne, East Sussex BN23 6NT, England

David C. Cook and the graphic circle C logo
are registered trademarks of Cook Communications Ministries.

The Web site addresses recommended throughout this book are offered as a resource to
you. These Web sites are not intended in any way to be or imply an endorsement on the
part of David C. Cook, nor do we vouch for their content.

Unless otherwise noted, all Scripture references are from the *Holy Bible, New
International Verison®*, *NIV®*. Copyright © 1973, 1978, 1984 by International Bible
Society. Used by permission of Zondervan. All rights reserved.

LCCN 2003267967
ISBN 978-0-7814-3805-6

Senior Editor: Janet Lee
Editor: Susan Martins Miller
Cover design: Andrea L. Boven
Interior design: Andrea L. Boven

Printed in the United States of America
First Edition 2002

3 4 5 6 7 8 9 10 11 12

092407

DEDICATION

To Carly, my precious granddaughter

Our times together are a treasure to my heart.
Whether talking, golfing, shopping, baking,
or enjoying our special island together,
our love is a gift to cherish.

Your tender heart toward God and all His creatures
inspires my own heart to be tender and sensitive.
How I praise God for you!
Love, Nan

CONTENTS

✲ ❋ ✲

LESSON GUIDES FOR MENTORS

ACKNOWLEDGMENTS

* ❋ *

Many thanks to Cook Communications Ministries for publishing *Appleseeds*. From the beginning, Cook embraced the vision for Apples of Gold and shared in the desire to minister to women through mentoring. With *Gifts of Gold* and *Appleseeds*, the Orchard is indeed growing. I am grateful for Cook's wisdom and support.

At the CORE of *Appleseeds*, are some very special women who helped make this book and program a special gift for 10-12 year old girls.

Susan Martins Miller is the truly gifted editor of *Appleseeds*. She helped me greatly to think pre-adolescent when I am, to say the least, 'post'. Susan's experience as managing editor for Godprints, a children's ministry line from Cook Communications Ministries, her work as an author of over 30 books, and her life as a mom of two gives her great insight. It has been a real treat to work with Susan and I pray that you will enjoy the fruit of our labor.

Sanibel Community Church, Sanibel Florida, sponsored a pilot for *Appleseeds* and helped fund it through their women's ministries. Mentors for the program were **Cille Gardner**, **Nancy Gerhard**, **Sandra Kyne**, and **Nancy Sampson**. Each of these women is also a mentor in the Sanibel Apples of Gold program. No woman could have dearer friends than these. Their love and encouragement are a precious gift to my heart.

Heather Corbin and **Linda Mondelli** were the project coordinators. Thanks Heather and Linda for the countless hours of planning and shopping for craft materials that would be appropriate for the lessons. We will all remember rag doll class 101.

To our very first Appleseeds—**Kristy Corbin**, **Rebecca Donovan**, **Meaghan Grinstead**, **Emma Halverson**, **Margie McDowell**, **Nina Mondelli**, **Crystal Robinson**, and **Brenna Williams**—thank you so very much. You were faithful in attendance and Bible study, joyful in attitude, and helpful with ideas. What fun it was to be with you and learn from you. I will always remember your sweet spirit. I pray that your love for the Lord will continue to grow and blossom and that you will stand tall for Jesus and be salt and light to the world around you. I also pray that the Lord will shower His blessings on your life.

Many thanks to **Janice Faber** for taking the songs of my heart from recorder to paper. Janice is an accomplished pianist with her own CD and is one of our 'polished apples'. And to **Jonathan De Cou**, Minister of Music at Central Wesleyan Church in Holland, thank you for typesetting the music for publication. Both Janice and Jonathan shared in this project with joy and enthusiasm and with a servant's heart. I am blessed to call them friends.

I thank the Lord so much for His faithfulness to the growing ministries of Apples of Gold. He is the true author of this ministry and deserves all the praise for its success. What a joy it is to put my hand in the Master's Hand and follow His words. He truly is the only AWESOME ONE!

GETTING STARTED

In 1995 God gave me a vision for a women's mentoring program that grew into Apples of Gold. This six-week nurturing program for women is based on two verses:

> A word aptly spoken is like apples of gold in a setting of silver (Proverbs 25:11).

> Teach the older women to be reverent in the way they live, not to be slanderers or addicted to much wine, but to teach what is good. Then they can train the younger women to love their husbands and children, to be self-controlled and pure, to be busy at home, to be kind, and to be subject to their husbands, so that no one will malign the word of God (Titus 2:3–5).

Soon after Apples of Gold started, participants began asking me to write a program for their daughters. I also began receiving mail asking how the class could be modified for girls. I'm delighted to respond to these requests with *Appleseeds*.

APPLESEEDS
MISSION STATEMENT

The purpose of *Appleseeds* is to teach girls how important they are to God, to their family and to others around them. We will teach that every person is created by God, in His image. The Bible says that each person is valuable to God and others. *Appleseeds* will seek to help each girl understand the person and work of God and how we can know Him personally. *Appleseeds* shows the relevancy of the Scriptures to our everyday lives and that serving God and others is a high calling.

Appleseeds will also teach that our lives should reflect the love of Christ. Each week we will learn that "Manners Matter" and good character is important. Each week a hands-on project will be a reminder of the Bible study for that week.

STARTING AN
APPLESEEDS CLASS

✳ ✳ ✳

Try to make participating in *Appleseeds* a free gift for the girls. The major costs will come in buying books for the girls and the craft supplies that you need each week. If you're associated with an Apples of Gold group, some of the women might like to make a generous gift so the *Appleseeds* girls can benefit from the same kind of nurturing relationships. You can ask parents to donate snacks if you'd like to serve something each week.

Your *Appleseeds* class has two important parts—the girls and the mentors. Gather mentors who are young at heart—and good listeners. They should be women whose lives shine for Jesus, who enjoy laughter, and who will get right down on the floor with the girls.

Each lesson has several different sections. Some mentors will be comfortable leading a Bible study, while others feel more gifted working with crafts or manners projects. That's okay! And the same person doesn't have to teach every lesson. Pray that the Lord will supply just the right mentors to teach the girls with love and enthusiasm. Plan on finding mentors other than the girls' mothers. I suggest you ask women whose own children are older, for instance. You may find that the girls relate beautifully with women who remind them of a Grammy. The most important thing mentors can do for your *Appleseeds* girls is pray for them—every day, by name.

The girls are the other important part of *Appleseeds*. If your ministry is church-based, you might have some girls who know the Bible fairly well and come from strong, caring homes. Don't forget to reach out to girls who may be on the outskirts of your congregation. You might also want to invite unchurched friends. An *Appleseeds* group is a wonderful way to help them feel valued and included. Be aware that girls come with "baggage," whether they're from a church family or the neighborhood. They may have attitudes or habits that are not at the top of your list! That's why they need *Appleseeds*.

If you can, hold your classes in a home. If you are familiar with the Apples of Gold program, you understand my desire to see our homes used to bring glory and honor to the Lord. The atmosphere is pleasant and cozy, making the girls feel comfortable and at ease. Meeting in homes also teaches the girls hospitality. If you hold classes in a church, try to bring a bit of home to your classes. Decorate some tables with pretty cloths and flowers. Try to meet in a cozy, quiet room where girls can sit in a small circle for their lesson.

Plan on about two hours for each lesson. Encourage the girls to prepare by reading and completing each week's lesson before you meet. Pages 108–137 of this book contain mentor guides for each of the lessons. Use a simple four-step plan to give structure and predictability to your time together.

Step 1: Life Craft

As the girls arrive, invite them to jump right into the craft. The mentors helping with the Life Craft will have a wonderful opportunity to spark conversation and build relationships.

Step 2: Bible Study Tips

The material on pages 15–107 of this book is for the girls to read and prepare in advance. The Bible study leader will want to prepare these pages as well in order to use them as a discussion guide. Digging for Seeds of Faith is optional for the girls, but you may want to make a point of using it in your discussion. The mentor planning pages include suggested answers. Each mentor's plan also includes ideas for captivating attention and enriching discussion.

Step 3: Manners Matter

Girls in this age group are hurtling toward independence. Help the girls find practical application of the Bible study topic, as well as build their confidence to face the world as gracious women of God. A terrific resource to have on hand is *Manners Matter* by Hermine Hartley and published by Barbour Publishing. Look for it at your local Christian bookstore, call Barbour Publishing at 1-800-847-8270, or visit www.barbourbooks.com.

Step 4: Wrapping Up

Close your time together each week with prayer and a song. Some lessons suggest an Apples of Gold song found at the back of this book. Make sure the girls have their crafts as they leave so they go out the door with a tangible reminder of what they've learned.

If this structure doesn't seem to be the best choice for your setting and group of girls, feel free to rearrange the lesson segments. The most important thing is the relationships between mentors and girls and the opportunity for girls to share what is on their hearts and minds.

When you've finished all the lessons, plan a special time to celebrate together. With the Appleseed girls' help, mentors will prepare a tea or lunch for the girls' moms. Include the girls with planning, preparing the food, setting the tables, and arranging centerpieces. When everything is ready, moms can join the celebration. Use the good dishes and linens. Treat the girls in a "grown up" way. Let them share favorite memories, whether hilarious or thought-provoking. Pass around photos. Celebrate the relationships that have sprouted up during your time together.

Also, I would love to hear how you adapted *Appleseeds*. Our website at www.applesofgold.org is a good place to exchange information with others involved in mentoring ministry. May God bless your *Appleseeds* ministry!

Betty Huizenga, 2002

APPLESEEDS

From appleseeds into lovely blossoms,
Purest white with frangrance sweet;
Filling the earth with grace and beauty.
God's perfect plan revealed in me.

From apple blossoms pure and fragrant
Into choice fruit so pleasant and sweet;
Clinging so closely to the branches.
God's perfect plan revealed in me.

I want to bear the fruit of the Spirit;
Fragrance of Jesus so precious and sweet;
Sharing His love to those all around me.
God's perfect plan revealed in me.

BETTY HUIZENGA, © 2002

LESSON ONE

Who Is God?

Now to the King eternal, immortal, invisible,
the only God, be honor and glory for ever and ever. Amen.
1 TIMOTHY 1:17

"Trust me. I know what's good for you." Maybe your mom or dad have said this to you, and even though you didn't like it, you knew it was true. But what if a stranger said this to you? Can you trust someone you don't know?

Think of three people you trust, and ask yourself why you trust those people. You'll probably decide that you trust people you know well. They love you and have treated you well. You trust people who care for you. You know that they want what's best for you.

If you had to explain what "trust" means to someone who didn't know the word, what would you say? Write your answer here:

____

____

____

____

No one knows what's best for you more than God does. But unless you know God, you might not be ready to trust Him. The Bible is our road map for knowing God so well that we'll trust Him with every part of our lives. The *Appleseeds* classes will help you discover what the Bible says about God and about you. Isn't it wonderful that the God who made us, the God who know us best, also tells us how to live with purpose, joy and peace?

Look up Genesis 1:1 and write it here:

_____

_____

_____

_____

God is the **Creator** of all things. He made everything on the earth—including you! What else can you learn about God from the first three words of the Bible: "In the beginning"?

Right from the beginning, God was there! God never wasn't. How's that for a brain teaser? God is **eternal.** He didn't have a beginning, and He'll never have an end. No person is eternal, just God. He will always be forever and ever the same God.

How does knowing that God is eternal make it easier for you to trust Him?

_____

_____

_____

_____

Eternity is a tough concept to understand. What does it mean for your faith? If God is eternal, then He'll always be there for you. You can trust Him because He will always be around to see you through any situation. Nothing can take God by surprise!

As your faith grows, you will learn that what God says is true. You will experience His working in your life, and your faith will grow until you know, without a doubt, that God is real and you will not be able to imagine life without Him. He will guide you and teach you. He will comfort you and help you. You can ask God the Father for everything you need. Because He made you, He cares deeply for you.

Look up Psalm 147:5 and write it here:

_____

_____

_____

_____

What does this verse tell us God is like?

_____

_____

_____

When you were little, did you ever try to count to infinity? At first you were sure you could do it if you just kept counting long enough. As you grew older, you realized that "infinity" truly has no end. That's what God is—**infinite.** You can probably think of some things that limit you. You're not old enough to drive a car, or not tall enough to reach the top cupboard, or not strong enough to move your dresser by yourself. You don't have enough time to play both soccer and softball. God doesn't have any of those limits. He's so big and everlasting that we have trouble even understanding what that means.

Now look up Revelation 4:8 and write it here:

_____

_____

_____

_____

What does this verse tell us God is like?

_____

_____

_____

_____

You've probably heard these words in a song. **Holy,** holy, holy! God is pure, perfect, sinless. That sets Him apart from humans. Everyone makes mistakes. But sometimes we choose to do what we know is wrong. The "blame game" started in the Garden of Eden with the very first mistake soon after God created humans. God told Adam and Eve that they could eat the fruit of any trees in the garden except one—the tree of knowledge of good and evil. So what tree did they eat from? That's right—the one tree that God told them to leave alone. You can read about this in Genesis 3.

When God asked Adam what he had done, Adam blamed Eve. Then Eve blamed the snake who told her that she could be like God if she ate that fruit. Have you ever played the "blame game"? Have you ever said, "It's not my fault! She made me do it!"

God never makes mistakes and He never sins. He wants us to grow more like Him, so that we can help other people know what God is like, too.

Look up Malachi 3:6 in the Old Testament and write it here:

_____

_____

_____

_____

What does this verse tell you about God?

_____

_____

_____

_____

God is **unchanging.** Maybe you've had a friend who changed the way she felt about you. Or maybe you drifted apart because your interests changed. God does not change! His love for you does not change. He is a friend you can trust without wondering if He will change His mind about you.

Creator. Eternal. Infinite. Holy. Unchanging. That's a pretty big picture of God, isn't it? God is awesome!

Write down some things that you think are awesome.

_____

_____

_____

_____

How is God even more awesome than any of those things?

_____

_____

_____

_____

You might be wondering why a God who is Creator, eternal, infinite, holy, and unchanging cares so much about you. After all, billions of people have lived on the earth. God is a **person**. He has feelings and thoughts, just as you do. He decides for himself what He wants to do, just as people do as they grow up. He wants to have relationships with the people He created, just as you want to have friendships with other people.

Genesis 1:27 says, "So God created man in his own image, in the image of God he created him; male and female he created them." What does it mean to you that God created you in His image?

_____

_____

_____

When God made you in His image, He gave you feelings and thoughts. He gave you the ability to decide for yourself what to believe and how to live. He made you so you could know Him and grow to be like Him. He wants to have a relationship with you. He wants you to trust Him and be close to Him.

He made you a person! You are as precious to God as if you were the only person He ever made! The more you know Him person to person, the more you'll want to trust Him.

In this lesson you learned about the bigness of God. You learned that this big God created you and wants to have a relationship with you. Learn more by looking up the verses in Digging for Seeds of Faith on pages 21–22.

How will what you've learned help your faith in God to grow? In your journal, answer this question:

 What seed of faith is planted in me today?

Remember that what you write in your journal is private and personal. You don't have to share it with anyone.

How awesome is the Lord Most High,
the great King over all the earth.

PSALM 47:2

* ❋ *

WHAT IS GOD LIKE?

Look up these verses in your Bible to learn more about God. Copy the verse here. Then write a word that summarizes what you learned about God from each verse.

Matthew 5:48

_____

_____

_____

_____

Psalm 139:7–12

_____

_____

_____

_____

Ezekiel 11:5

_____

_____

_____

Psalm 145:9

_____

_____

_____

Psalm 111:7

_____

_____

_____

1 John 2:1

_____

_____

_____

Daniel 9:9

_____

_____

_____

✳ ✺ ✳

HOW CAN I KNOW GOD?

*Jesus Christ is the same yesterday
and today and forever.*

HEBREWS 13:8

If God created us, loves us and wants a relationship with us, why doesn't everyone love God? Remember the "blame game" from the Garden of Eden? When God made us in His image, He made us so we can make choices of our own free will. Adam and Eve doubted what God had said and believed the serpent instead. They chose sin. After that, humans didn't have the same relationship with God any more.

Does that mean that God stopped loving them? No. And He doesn't stop loving you when you sin and make mistakes. Remember, God is a person and wants relationships. As much as our holy God hates sin, He loves the people who sin. He wants to help them stop sinning and have the right kind of relationship with Him.

What do Adam and Eve have to do with you? Find out by reading Romans 3:23. Write the verse here:

_____

_____

_____

What do you think it means to "fall short of the glory of God"?

_____

_____

_____

_____

Sin is disobedience to God. We know when we have done wrong. Our conscience tells us. Like dirty dishes, our lives need to be washed, perhaps even scrubbed clean, so that we can have the kind of relationship with God that He wants to have with us.

Find Romans 5:8 in your Bible and write the verse here:

_____

_____

_____

_____

What does this verse say that God did for us? Why?

_____

_____

_____

_____

Think of all the people you love. You might be thinking of people who are kind to you, give you gifts, spend time with you and do what you like to do. It's one thing to love someone who is nice and kind; it's harder to love someone who is mean or grouchy or does things that hurt you. That's what God does. God is **loving.** He loves us even when we disobey His commandments and hurt Him. God's love is perfect and His love never fails. God says, "I have loved you with an everlasting love" (Jeremiah 31:3).

Have you ever been angry with someone you love? Sure! Maybe your little brother or sister broke something that was important to you.

Maybe your mom or dad hurt your feelings. Maybe your best friend lied to you. God understands how you feel.

Read Psalm 145:8 and write it here:

_____

_____

_____

_____

How does God handle anger with someone He loves?

_____

_____

_____

What do you think it means to be compassionate? Check the dictionary if you're not sure. God is **compassionate.** He cares about you and how you feel, even when you do something that hurts Him.

God doesn't stop with just knowing how you feel or loving you even if He has reason to be angry. His love turns into action.

Look up Daniel 9:9 and write it here:

_____

_____

_____

"Mercy" is not a word we use very much these days. God is **merciful.** This means that God doesn't give us what we deserve. Now read Hebrews 8:12 and write it here:

_____

_____

_____

After mercy, the next way God turns His love into action is to be **forgiving**. He's perfect, righteous, and holy. But He understands us. He cares about our needs and hurts. He doesn't give us the punishment we deserve for our sin. Instead, He forgives us. When God forgives us, He doesn't remember our sin anymore. It's really gone!

When you forgive a friend or a friend forgives you, then you have a small picture of what forgiveness really means. God is the only one who can forgive all our sin—even the ones no one else knows about—so that we can have the right kind of relationship with Him. God shows His mercy and doesn't give us the punishment we deserve. Instead, Jesus took that punishment, and God forgives us!

Here's a verse that you may know by memory!

> For God so loved the world that he gave his one and only Son,
> that whoever believes in him shall not perish,
> but have eternal life.
> John 3:16

This is one of the first verses from the Bible that people memorize. That's because it sums up the story of God's love and forgiveness. This familiar verse tells us the essence of who Jesus is and why He came to earth. Believing that verse and taking it personally is the most important decision you will ever make in your *entire* life. It guarantees your future in heaven with Jesus, but it also gives you a fuller life on earth.

Have you ever said to someone, "I forgive you, but I won't forget what you did to me?" Do you think that is true forgiveness? How would you feel if God forgave, but did not forget?

Some people think that they've been so bad that no one can forgive them, not even God! Find out what God says in 1 John 1:9 and write it here:

_____

_____

_____

What does this verse say is your part?

_____

_____

_____

If you've ever seen a snowfall on a crystal clear evening, you know it's a beautiful sight to see. Each snowflake sparkles in the light. Or perhaps you have awakened to a snowy morning and seen the sun shining down on the new-fallen snow. What an incredible sight! God's forgiveness is like that—a clean, fresh start.

Read John 1:12 and write it here:

_____

_____

_____

_____

What does it mean to be a child of God?

_____

_____

_____

_____

God wants you to know Him in your heart, and not just in your mind. That's why He sent Jesus to earth to die on the cross and take the punishment we deserve. That's why He wants us to be His children.

"Everybody else is doing it!" Have you ever tried to use that excuse for doing something that you knew was wrong? It probably didn't work with your parents or teachers! And it doesn't work with God either. You can't distract God from your sin by pointing at what everyone else is doing.

Or did you think that because God is so nice, He'll let you off the hook? God is kind, but He isn't soft. In kindness He takes us firmly by the hand and shows us the life He wants us to live. Then He makes it possible for us to live that life because of what Jesus did for us.

We can't do anything, in our own strength, to be good enough to be a child of God. It's a gift that God gives us. If you're ready to accept this gift, you can pray a prayer like this one:

> Dear Jesus, I believe You are the Son of God and that You died on the cross to save me from my sins. I know that I sin against You, and You are the only one who can forgive me. Please come into my life and forgive me. Help me to know You better and show my love for You by obeying what You want me to do. In Your name I pray. Amen.

In this lesson you discovered how you can know the King of Kings personally. You learned that God sent Jesus to be your Savior so that you can accept God's forgiveness. By believing in Jesus, you become a child of the King. You can learn more about what believers through the centuries have thought about God by working thru Digging for Seeds of Faith on pages 29–31.

How will what you've learned help your faith in God to grow? In your journal, answer this question:

 What seed of faith is planted in me today?

Remember that what you write in your journal is private and personal. You don't have to share it with anyone.

Your faithfulness continues through all generations;
you established the earth and it endures.
PSALM 119:90

THE APOSTLES' CREED

Church leaders in the second century wrote the words to the Apostles' Creed. They wanted a clear statement of what Christians believe the Bible teaches and nothing else. Nearly 2,000 years later, many congregations still say the Apostles' Creed together to remind themselves what they believe.

Read each part of the Apostles' Creed. Then write what it means in your own words.

I believe in God, the Father, Almighty, Maker of heaven and earth,

_____

_____

_____

_____

and in Jesus Christ, His only begotten Son, our Lord, who was conceived by the Holy Spirit, born of the virgin Mary,

_____

_____

_____

_____

suffered under Pontius Pilate, was crucified, dead and buried. He descended into hell. The third day, He arose again from the dead.

_____

_____

_____

_____

He ascended into heaven and is seated at the right hand of God the Father.

_____

_____

_____

_____

From there He will come to judge the living and the dead.

_____

_____

_____

_____

I believe in the Holy Spirit,

_____

_____

_____

_____

the holy catholic church, (This refers to all believers everywhere, not any particular faith.)

_____

_____

_____

the forgiveness of sins,

_____

_____

_____

_____

the communion of the Saints,

_____

_____

_____

_____

the resurrection of the body, and life everlasting.

_____

_____

_____

_____

WHO AM I?

You created my inmost being;
you knit me together in my mother's womb.

PSALM 139:13

Who Am I?

Who am I anyway?
Where do I belong?
Though I try to do what's right,
I seem to do what's wrong.
Who am I anyway?
Does anybody care
What I think or feel or say?
Is anybody there?

You are made in My own image,
I have known you from the start,
I know everything about you, and
I know what's in your heart.

I have found it is true
Jesus cares for me.
I asked Him into my heart
He has set me free.

Now I know who I am,
No more wondering
I'm a child of Jesus now—
A child of the King!
BETTY HUIZENGA, © 2001

Have you ever imagined the throne room of a palace? What do you think a throne room looks like? A large room, full of beautiful things? Perhaps you see a beautiful crystal chandelier, and perhaps you imagine a long red carpet leading up to the throne. Or perhaps it is purple or gold.

The throne room is where a king receives special visitors. As you enter, the king sits on his throne, dressed in his royal robes and wearing his jewel-filled crown. His throne is higher than the floor and steps lead up to the throne. You walk to the foot of the throne and bow down before the king to show respect.

A human king may not want to see you. You might not even get into the throne room, or once you are there the king may not want to listen to you.

Now imagine this. In the throne room of the King of Kings you are always welcome, and, even more remarkable, He is eager for you to enter. You do not need an appointment, no need for a servant to introduce you. The Kings of Kings already knows your name. He knows if you have a problem at home or with a friend. He knows if you are having a tough time at school with a teacher or your homework.

Not only does God know all about you, but He cares. You are His child and He is the perfect heavenly Father. He says, "Come to me. I will listen. I will help."

Look up Isaiah 6:1–3 in your Bible. Write down some key words.

_____

_____

_____

Seraphs are a kind of angel. It may be hard to picture what they really look like, but we do know what their job is—praising God as He sits on his throne. Angels are not the only ones who can praise the King of Kings. Let's look at a special chapter of the Bible that helps us understand why we should praise God too.

Find Psalm 139 in your Bible. The Book of Psalms is right smack in the middle of the Bible. Read Psalm 139:1–6. Write down three ideas about God that you see in these verses.

1.

_____

_____

2.

_____

_____

3.

_____

_____

When you go to school, God is with you. He knows about the test you must take, or report you must finish "yesterday." When you're with your best friend, God is with you. He knows all your thoughts. He knows about the person who is unkind to you and how tough it can be to be included as a friend.

Now read Psalm 139:7–12. What word pictures about your relationship with God do you find in these verses?

1.

_____

_____

_____

2.

_____

_____

_____

3.

_____

_____

_____

Can you imagine that God knows what you are going to say before you do? Can you imagine that there is not a single place you can hide from God? If you are close to God, these words are a great comfort. If you are trying to hide from God, these words might bother you.

If God is with you everywhere you go and knows your every thought, how does that change your decisions about what to say and do?

_____

_____

_____

Read the next part of the psalm, verses 13–16. What response does God want from us for the way that He made us?

_____

_____

_____

_____

Perhaps your mom or "Grammy" is a knitter. With just a couple of needles and some yarn, she can create a beautiful sweater. How can a straight piece of yarn become an intricate, colorful sweater full of interesting patterns? It is made one stitch at a time with great care. If the knitter makes a mistake, she must correct it, or the quality and strength of the finished sweater will be flawed.

God says He made you in that way. He knitted you together, stitch by stitch, into a beautiful, flawless pattern that is unique. There will never be another you! You may resemble your mom or sister, but you are not exactly like either of them. You have your own DNA, your own fingerprint, your own personality. You are the only *you*. You are special, made just right by God Himself.

We cannot fathom the mind of God. We cannot understand how He can create millions of people and no two are exactly alike. What an incredible, awesome God He is!

Write down three phrases that you like to use to praise God for the way He made you. Try to think of one you've never said before!

When you enter the throne room of God, you stand before the Creator who made you with love and care and who is with you always. When you are God's child, He wants you to bring all your needs and concerns to Him.

Read 1 Peter 5:7 and write the verse here:

_____

_____

_____

_____

God loves you so much. He cares about every detail of your life. He wants to help you, to guide you and make you feel secure in Him.

Now read Hebrews 4:16 and write it here:

_____

_____

_____

Imagine that! You can approach God's throne with confidence. He is King of Kings, and yet you can approach Him and know that He will give help.

Perhaps you feel that you don't know how to pray to God. Start by getting ready to be with God. Read Psalm 46:10. What does this verse tell you to do?

_____

_____

_____

Be ready to listen, not just to talk. Sometimes Jesus calls God's children "sheep." Read John 10:27, 28. What can we learn from sheep about how to pray?

_____

_____

_____

Sheep follow the shepherd's voice. God speaks to our hearts through the Holy Spirit. If you are listening, you will surely hear Him. Sometimes we are impatient, but God has His own time schedule. He is never early or late with His answer. He may test your patience, but He is perfectly patient. He may answer in a way you think is not best, but His answer will be perfect for you. He wants you to come to His throne often and stay a long time.

Have you ever seen a dog in a car with its head out the window, ears flapping in the wind? The car goes faster, the dog's ears are pinned back, and no matter what you say, that dog can't hear you! When you hurry through life, it's like your ears are pressed back in the wind. You cannot listen to God or anyone else. But when you stop and take time to be still, you can listen much better.

The end of Psalm 139 is the heart of the chapter. Read verses 23 and 24. Can you honestly pray those words to your Heavenly Father? What will God find when He searches your heart? What anxious thoughts will God find in your heart? What "offensive ways" will He find?

What does verse 24 say God will do for you if you open your heart to Him?

_____

_____

Into your throne room I'm coming,
Humbly I bow before your throne,
Seeking to know your grace and wisdom,
Yielding my spirit to your own.

Teach me to listen when you call me.
Give me a heart that's warm and kind,
Reaching outside my place of comfort,
Helping the sick, the lame, the blind.

Teach me to love as you have loved me.
May all my life reflect your grace,
Your Holy Spirit's power within me,
All earthly doubt and fear erase.

And when my days on earth are ended,
Before your throne my knee shall bow.
I want to hear, "Well done, my servant,
Enter My heavenly kingdom now."

BETTY HUIZENGA, © 2000

In this lesson you've explored one of the most famous passages in the Bible. You've learned that the King of Kings made you, and you can come to Him at anytime—no appointment needed! You can know more about how to approach the throne of grace with confidence by digging into Digging for Seeds of Faith on page 40–41.

How will what you've learned help your faith in God to grow? In your journal, answer this question:

 What seed of faith is planted in me today?

Remember that what you write in your journal is private and personal. You don't have to share it with anyone.

My mouth will speak in praise of the Lord.
Let every creature praise his holy name for ever and ever.

PSALMS 145:21

APPROACHING THE THRONE

Even though you are always welcome in God's throne room, don't just barge in. You would never do that to a king. Come with respect and reverence before His throne. Remember He is holy! Here is a pattern you can follow to pray. Read the heading for each section, then write your own words to express what you could say in that part of your prayer.

Address God.

Begin by saying "Heavenly Father" or "Dear Jesus." What else could you say to begin a prayer?

_____

_____

_____

Praise God.

Praise Him for one of His attributes that you have learned about. List some ideas you could use:

_____

_____

_____

_____

Confess your sin to God.

Tell Him you are sorry for your sin. Be specific about sin you're sorry for.

Make your requests known to God.

Philippians 4:6 says, "Do not be anxious about anything, but in everything, by prayer and petition, with thanksgiving, present your requests to God. And the peace of God, which transcends all understanding, will guard your hearts and your minds in Christ Jesus."

What kinds of things can you ask God for?

_____

_____

_____

Listen to God.

God listens to you, but He wants to speak to you as well. Think about some things that you need to listen to God about.

_____

_____

_____

Thank God.

1 Thessalonians 5:16 says, "Be joyful always; pray continually; give thanks in all circumstances for this is God's will for you in Christ Jesus." Make a list of things you can thank God for.

_____

_____

_____

Are you beginning to see the difference between an earthly king and a heavenly king? Whose child would you rather be?

✳

WHAT AM I THINKING?

Whatever is true, whatever is noble, whatever is right,
whatever is pure, whatever is lovely, whatever is admirable,
if anything is excellent or praiseworthy, think about such things.

PHILIPPIANS 4:8

Do you ever daydream?

Do you have a wonderful imagination?

Do you love learning how things work?

Doctors and scientists have learned a lot about how the brain works. But they can't explain everything about the human mind. For instance, think about your memory. What is your earliest memory? How old were you? How amazing our memory is. If you looked at old photos with your mom or grandma, you might be surprised at what she remembers—the color of a dress in a black and white photo, how old she was on that trip to the beach, even the cold peas at Thanksgiving dinner. The clothes and the food are long gone, but the memories remain.

What precious memories do you have? Write some of them in your journal this week. They will become a treasure to your heart.

Perhaps you also have some painful memories. You would love to erase them from your mind, but you can't. God can forgive and forget, but we have a harder time forgetting painful things. With the Lord's help, these memories can become less painful.

Every day you see new things, hear new things, experience new things. Your eyes and ears and nose and hands all bring new information to your brain. You're learning all the time, whether you realize it or not! But how does what you learn affect you? What kind of ideas are going into your mind?

Romans 8:5–8 tells us that thinking about ourselves all the time leads to a dead end. When we set our minds on just what we want, and not what God wants, we end up working against God. But if we set our minds on doing what God wants, we please God.

Read Romans 12:2 and write it here:

_____

_____

_____

_____

What "patterns of this world" do you see in your everyday life?

_____

_____

_____

_____

What happens when God transforms your mind?

_____

_____

_____

_____

It's hard to control what you think about! In a split millisecond, the picture you see on television becomes a picture in your mind. And when someone hurts you, your feelings are hard to get off your mind. But God, who created you, can renew your mind and help you think about the right things.

What are the right things to think about? Read Philippians 4:8 and find out. Then give your own short definition and example of each word.

True

_____

_____

_____

_____

Noble

_____

_____

_____

_____

Right

_____

_____

_____

_____

Pure

_____

_____

_____

_____

Lovely

_____

_____

_____

_____

Admirable

_____

_____

_____

Excellent

_____

_____

_____

Praiseworthy

_____

_____

_____

Now go back and put a check mark next to any words that describe thoughts that you've had in the last few days.

Jesus said, "Love the Lord your God with all your heart and with all your soul and with all your mind (Matthew 22:37). This means being careful about what thoughts you let live in your mind. Give God your thoughts, and let Him fill your mind with His Spirit.

God's Word gives us lots of help with the kind of thoughts God wants us to have. When Solomon became king of God's people, he knew that he would need God's help to be a wise leader. God said, "Ask for whatever you want," and Solomon asked for wisdom to tell the difference between right and wrong (1 Kings 3:9). King Solomon went on to write the Book of Proverbs, a book full of God's wisdom. At the beginning of the book, Solomon tells us the purpose:

1. for attaining wisdom and discipline;
2. for understanding words of insight;
3. for acquiring a disciplined and prudent life, doing what is right and just and fair;
4. for giving prudence to the simple, knowledge and discretion to the young.

Another word for "prudence" is "common sense." And discretion is knowing when to be careful about what you say and who you say it to. A wise person knows how to control his or her words. It's easy to make mistakes about basic things in our lives. God wants you to understand the basic things and apply His wisdom to them.

The best thing about wisdom is that we don't have to find it on our own. Look up James 1:5–7 and write it here:

_____

_____

_____

_____

Close your eyes for a moment and picture the ocean. Imagine waves swept high by the wind. Picture a beach ball on the waves. It bounces all around—tossed to and fro by the wind. God doesn't want your faith to be like that. He gives wisdom when you need it.

God's wisdom in your life will help you avoid trouble. As you grow older, you'll make more and more decisions on your own. Good judgment, or discernment, means knowing when to say "No," not because your parents said so, but because you understand right and wrong in your own heart.

Make a list of five choices that you've made today. Think about what you ate, words you spoke, how you spent your time, how you spent money, or what you've read.

1.

_____

_____

_____

2.

_____

_____

_____

3.

_____

_____

_____

4.

_____

_____

_____

5.

_____

_____

_____

God created you with a mind, and He wants you to use your mind to make wise choices. Let's explore some choices that please God.

Proverbs 20:11 says, "Even a child is known by his actions, by whether his conduct is pure and right." What good choice does this verse tell you God wants you to make?

_____

_____

_____

_____

God wants you to be a person of integrity. That means that what you say and do shows what is really in your heart. No matter what you say you think or believe, your actions will tell the truth.

1 Thessalonians 5:15 says, "Make sure that nobody pays back wrong for wrong, but always try to be kind to each other and to everyone." What good choice does this verse tell you God wants you to make?

_____

_____

_____

_____

Mark, a child with Downs Syndrome, went with his mother to McDonald's for lunch one day. A family with two children sat in the next booth. At first the children stared at Mark, then they began to make faces. Their parents never stopped them. Mark stopped eating, and his eyes teared up. His mom took him out to the car to finish his lunch.

How do you react to someone who looks different or has a different background than your own?

Do you ever wonder what love looks like? First Corinthians 13 is called the "love chapter" of the Bible. It paints a good picture of what love should look like. The last verse of the chapter says, "Now these three remain: faith, hope and love. But the greatest of these is love." What good choice does this chapter tell you God wants you to make?

_____

_____

_____

Loving others isn't always easy. Sometimes you're angry with your parents or annoyed with your brothers and sisters. Sometimes your friends disappoint you. But in this passage, the Apostle Paul tells us that love is the most important choice we can make.

You might think that some of the choices you make right now don't matter very much. Find out what God's Word says. Read Proverbs 3:21, 22 and write the verses here:

_____

_____

_____

_____

What kinds of things might make you lose sight of good judgment?

_____

_____

_____

_____

Do you have a favorite necklace? Maybe it's one that feels good to wear. Maybe it's one that other people notice and comment on. Good judgment is "an ornament to grace your neck," like a necklace or a beautiful garland. You know what it means to you to wear it, and when others notice it, they see the beauty as well.

In this lesson you've learned how important it is to be careful about what influences your mind. And you've seen how what's in your mind influences the choices you make. You can learn more about how God wants you to use your mind. Turn to Digging for Seeds of Faith on page 51–53.

How will what you've learned help your faith in God to grow? In your journal, answer this question:

 What seed of faith is planted in me today?

Remember that what you write in your journal is private and personal. You don't have to share it with anyone.

❋

*You will keep him in perfect peace whose mind is steadfast,
because he trusts in you.*

ISAIAH 26:3

CHOICES THAT PLEASE GOD

Look up these verses and write down the choices that God wants you to make.

Ephesians 6:1
God wants me to choose to

_____

_____

_____

Proverbs 1:8, 9
God wants me to choose to

_____

_____

_____

Hebrews 12:14
God wants me to choose to

_____

_____

_____

_____

Ephesians 4:32
God wants me to choose to

_____

_____

_____

Psalm 37:4
God wants me to choose to

_____

_____

_____

1 Thessalonians 5:18
God wants me to choose to

_____

_____

_____

Proverbs 3:5, 6
God wants me to choose to

_____

_____

_____

_____

John 14:23

God wants me to choose to

_____

_____

_____

_____

Write about one choice that you will make to please God this week.

_____

_____

_____

_____

WHAT AM I LOOKING AT?

Keep me as the apple of your eye;
hide me in the shadow of your wings.

PSALM 17:8

How many magazines have you looked at this week? How much time have you spent on the internet or in front of the television? Or have you been out shopping and looking at new clothes? Did you notice your friend's new sweater or the poster of her favorite musical group? Your eyes have been busy!

Our eyesight is a precious gift from God. When God created us, He protected our eyes in many ways. Notice how the bones of your skull come around the eye for protection. God also gave us eyelashes and eyebrows to keep the dirt from our eyes. We all know how painful it is to have something in our eye, and how we just can't wait to get it out. Tear ducts keep our eyes moistened and healthy.

Now look up Matthew 6:23 and write it here:

_____

_____

_____

_____

In addition to talking about good eyesight, what other meaning does this verse have?

As light comes into your eyes, you see things clearly. It is difficult to see clearly in the darkness. Perhaps you have taken a tour into a cave. You follow the guide and carry flashlights. You can find your way into the darkness of the cave. Once you are all deep into the cave, the guide tells you about the wonders of the cave, then he asks the tourists to turn the flashlights off. The darkness is overwhelming. It can be pretty scary. What a relief when the lights come back on.

In John 8:12, Jesus says, "I am the light of the world. Whoever follows me will never walk in darkness, but will have the light of life." Jesus gives light to the whole world. You don't ever have to go through a dark time alone. Jesus is with you, showing you God's way. And the better you know God, the more you will reflect His light to the people around you.

Read Psalm 119:105 and write it here:

_____

_____

_____

_____

God's Word guides us through our life, shedding light to show us where to go. His light also shines through us to other people.

What do people see when they look at you? Write out 1 Peter 3:3–5.

_____

_____

_____

_____

This verse doesn't mean it's wrong to make your hair pretty or wear a bracelet or ring. But it does remind us that true beauty comes from what's in the inside, not what's on the outside. You probably look in a mirror several times a day to fix your hair or check your clothes or maybe even put on a little make-up. If you do those things, when other people see you, they know that you care about how you look. You can use God's Word as a "mirror" to see what's on the inside.

Do you remember the story of how God chose David to be the king of His people? You can read about it in 1 Samuel 16. First Samuel looked at all of David's older brothers. The oldest brother was tall and handsome, and Samuel thought he would be a good king. But God told Samuel that God does not look at how a person appears on the outside. He looks at the person's heart. David was just a shepherd boy, but God liked what He saw in David's heart, and He chose David to be king.

Look up these verses and make a list of things that God wants you to have on the inside.

- Proverbs 15:13

_____

_____

_____

_____

- Proverbs 15:30

_____

_____

_____

_____

- Proverbs 17:22

_____

_____

_____

_____

- Proverbs 31:25

_____

_____

_____

_____

- Proverbs 31:30

_____

_____

_____

_____

Think about three women you admire. What are the qualities that make you want to be like these women? List them here.

_____

_____

_____

_____

If you decided you wanted to be just like one of these women, what's the first thing you would do? Perhaps you would dress the way she dresses. Maybe you would talk the way she talks. Or maybe you would prepare for the same kind of career that she has. Or would it be more important to notice how she treats other people and shows the light of Jesus to the world?

How you treat other people shows what kind of light is inside of you. If we're honest with ourselves, we can all admit to making a snap judgment about someone else. Maybe you've experienced one of these situations:

- deciding you don't like another person before you get to know the person well.

- judging someone else by outward appearance, not what's on the inside.
- being rude to someone who is not as cool and popular as you want to be.
- laughing at someone just because everyone else is laughing.
- ignoring someone who wants you for a friend.

If you've been treated this way, then you know it doesn't feel good! Jesus is the light of the world. Those who follow Jesus walk in His light. They can see what they're doing and where they're going. They reflect His light to the people around them.

Look up Philippians 2:14, 15 and write the words here:

_____

_____

_____

_____

If we didn't have mathematicians and scientists to tell us, it would be hard to imagine how far away the stars are. The Apostle Paul wrote these words centuries before humans tried to measure the distance between earth and stars. He didn't need to know how far away they were to know how powerful the light of a star is. A star's light shines in the blackness of the night sky all the way down to earth, billions of miles away. God wants you to shine like that! If you get away from city lights on a clear night and look at the sky, the longer you look, the more stars you'll see. Imagine a universe filled with the light of people who are following Jesus!

Good news! You don't have to do all this on your own. Look up Hebrews 12:2, 3 and write the words here:

_____

_____

_____

God's Word tells you exactly where to look—at Jesus. Read the stories in the Bible of how Jesus treated other people. Read what Jesus taught the people of his day about what God wants to see on the inside. And remember that Jesus is the one who gives you your faith. He's the one who will keep you strong. He's the "author and perfecter" of our faith, and He will not let you grow weary.

Think about your eyes in a new way. Look through your eyes to see what God sees in your heart. Look through your eyes to see what God sees in other people. And look at Jesus, who will keep your faith strong.

The psalmist prayed, "Keep me as the apple of your eye; hide me in the shadow of your wings" (Psalm 17:8). What part of the eye would you say is the "apple"? The pupil or ball of the eye is most precious. We want to protect and care for it. The psalmist reminds us that we can call on God to help us and give us the protection we need.

What does Proverbs 7:2 say? Write it here:

_____

_____

_____

_____

In this lesson you've learned that God wants us to be as careful to follow his teachings as we are to take care of our eyes. You've seen how what you look at with your eyes shows what's in your heart. And you've seen how you can be a light shining for others to see Jesus in you.

You can learn more about how God wants you to use your eyes by working through Digging for Seeds of Faith on pages 61–62.

How will what you've learned help your faith in God to grow? In your journal, answer this question:

What seed of faith is planted in me today?

Remember that what you write in your journal is private and personal. You don't have to share it with anyone.

Man looks at the outward appearance,
but the Lord looks at the heart.

1 SAMUEL 16:7

EYES OF THE HEART

Look up these verses and write down how God wants you to use your eyes to please him.

Psalm 19:8

_____

_____

_____

Psalm 25:15

_____

_____

_____

Psalm 118:23

_____

_____

_____

_____

Psalm 141:8

_____

_____

_____

_____

Proverbs 17:24

_____

_____

_____

_____

Psalm 121:1

_____

_____

_____

_____

Ephesians 1:18

_____

_____

_____

_____

* ❋ *

WHAT AM I LISTENING TO?

He who answers before listening—
that is his folly and his shame.

PROVERBS 18:13

"Pay attention!"

"Listen carefully! I'm only going to say this once."

"Are you hearing a word I'm saying?"

"I'm talking to you!"

Can you hear your parents saying things like this? Or a teacher at school, or your Sunday school teacher? They want you to listen! Getting someone's attention is not always easy. Perhaps you've had the experience of giving a presentation to your class, and other kids were talking or moving around while you were presenting. Or maybe you've helped with a class of younger kids at church. If you have, you know how hard it is to get everyone's attention at the same time.

But just hearing someone's words is not the end of true listening. Here is what James 1:22-25 says about listening:

Do not merely listen to the word, and so deceive yourselves. Do what it says. Anyone who listens to the word but does not do what it says is like a man who looks at his face in a mirror and, after looking at himself, goes away and immediately forgets what he looks like. But the man who looks intently into the perfect law that gives freedom, and continues to do this, not forgetting what he has heard, but doing it—he will be blessed in what he does.

How do you deceive yourself if you listen to the Word of God but do not do what it says?

_____

_____

_____

God says it is important that we listen to His Word. The Bible has 66 books, and every one of them has some wisdom from God. King Solomon asked God for wisdom. He wrote the Book of Proverbs. A "proverb" is a wise saying. The Book of Proverbs is full of wisdom for everyday living.

Read each of these verses, then write what you learn about listening and wisdom from each verse.

Proverbs 4:7–9

_____

_____

_____

_____

Proverbs 1:5

_____

_____

_____

_____

Proverbs 2:1–5

_____

_____

_____

_____

Proverbs 2:4 says to search for wisdom as a hidden treasure. There are still places out West where you can "pan" for gold. People go out to the riverbeds with screens and pails. They drag the bottom of the river searching for even the tiniest piece of gold. They put the water mixture through a strainer and remove any particles of gold they find.

God says we are to search in that way for wisdom. Look for it everywhere, take even the smallest bit of wisdom, and examine it for the "golden nuggets." God's Word is full of these precious nuggets. Once you learn what they mean, they will be in your heart for the rest of your life.

Read Proverbs 22:17, 18 and write it here:

_____

_____

_____

_____

What is the main idea you can learn from these verses?

_____

_____

_____

_____

Memorize Scripture and have the verses ready on your lips! You'll never know when the words will come to mind at just the right time. A young girl memorized Psalm 8, a wonderful psalm about the majesty of God. Decades later, she drove across a bridge toward an island in a convertible. The island was dark ahead, the moon was full, and the stars exploded with light everywhere. Out of her heart came the words she had learned as a child. Tears came to her eyes as her husband joined her in proclaiming the wonders of God's love.

> O Lord, Our Lord,
> How majestic is your name in all the earth!
>
> When I consider your heavens, the work of your fingers,
> the moon and the stars,
> which you have set in place,
> What is man that you are mindful of him,
> the son of man that you care for him?
> You made him a little lower than the heavenly beings,
> And crowned him with glory and honor.
>
> O Lord, our Lord,
> How majestic is your name in all the earth!

Majestic means grand in size, beauty, or worth. It's a very "kingly" description. What's your favorite song about the majesty of Jesus?

Did you know that listening to God is good for your health? Read Proverbs 3:1 and find out how.

_____

_____

_____

_____

When we follow God's way, we make wiser decisions. We may have longer life and better health because we understand that God created our bodies and we need to care for them. For instance, by deciding not to smoke, drink alcohol or use drugs, we can help keep our bodies healthier. The decisions you make about listening to God will affect your entire life. Listen to Him!

How do you really feel about getting advice? Do you listen to advice, or do you say, "Don't tell me what to do!" Your response may depend on the person giving the advice. It's easier to accept advice from someone you love and respect. Many voices call for your attention every day: friends, advertisements, television shows, magazines. Not every piece of advice you hear is good for you. God wants to give you the wisdom to know the difference so that you can choose His way in every situation.

For instance, in your opinion, is it okay to listen to songs with questionable or bad words in them? How about listening to off-color jokes or stories? What do you do when those around you use bad words, words that curse the name of God? Maybe some of your friends do these things. Decide today that you will not have any part in cursing the name of God, or cursing other people. Promise yourself that you will not use God's name in a way that does not bring honor to Him.

Or suppose you get into an argument with someone in your family or with a friend. How can listening to God's wisdom help you in that situation? Write James 1:19 here:

_____

_____

_____

_____

Usually in an argument, you want to do the talking! You're trying to get your point across. But James tells us to be quick to listen, slow to speak and slow to become angry. That's practical advice from God's Word that you can use every day.

When you listen to God's wisdom, you get to know Him better. Remember, God created you so that you could have a relationship with Him. He wants you to talk to him. The Almighty God, Creator of the whole universe, hears you when you call.

Have you ever cried in your pillow, thinking no one would hear you? God hears you crying in your pillow and He knows why you are crying. What a comfort! Talk to Him with your whole heart; tell Him all your needs. He doesn't need to talk with anyone else or seek advice from anyone else. He has the answers.

Write out Psalm 34:11:

_____

_____

_____

_____

Write out Psalm 34:15:

_____

_____

_____

_____

You can see in these words how much God wants you to come to Him. His ears are listening to you, and He wants to teach you.

God cares when a nation calls on Him as well. He cares about our country and the world He created. Here is what 2 Chronicles 7:14 says:

If my people, who are called by my name, will humble themselves and pray and seek my face and turn from their wicked ways, then will I hear from heaven and will forgive their sin and will heal their land.

What does God ask the people to do?

_____

_____

_____

_____

How does God respond when the people call on Him?

_____

_____

_____

God is listening. Are you?

In this lesson you've learned that God wants you to listen to the wisdom that comes from His Word. You've seen how the advice you listen to helps make your life better. And you've seen that God listens when you call out to Him.

You can learn more about how God wants you to use your ears, and the ears of your heart. Turn to Digging for Seeds of Faith on pages 70–71.

How will what you've learned help your faith in God to grow? In your journal, answer this question:

 What seed of faith is planted in me today?

Remember that what you write in your journal is private and personal. You don't have to share it with anyone.

Listen, my son, and be wise,
and keep your heart on the right path.
PROVERBS 23:19

EARS OF THE HEART

God gives you people to help you learn to listen to Him. He asks you to obey and honor our parents and others who have authority over you. Even Jesus, the Savior, submitted to His earthly parents. In Luke 2:49–51 we read the story of Jesus in the temple. He was listening to the teachers in the temple and asking questions, but His parents didn't know where He was for three days. After they found Him, verse 51 says, "Then Jesus went down to Nazareth with them, and was obedient to them."

Read these verses and write down the reasons you should pay attention to the people who have responsibility for you.

God wants me to pay attention because...

Proverbs 1:8

_____

_____

_____

Proverbs 8:32, 33

_____

_____

_____

_____

Jeremiah 29:11

_____

_____

_____

_____

Ephesians 5:21

_____

_____

_____

_____

James 3:17, 18

_____

_____

_____

_____

* ✳ *

May 9
Bennie
Apple muffins
Laurie

WHAT AM I SAYING?

*A word fitly spoken is like apples of gold
in settings of silver.*

PROVERBS 25:11

"What is down in the well comes up in the bucket." Have you ever heard that saying? It isn't hard to figure out what it means. If the well is full of crystal clear water, that's what comes out of it. If the well is full of muddy water, that's what comes out of it.

Your heart is like a well, and your mouth is the bucket. What comes out of your mouth shows what is in your heart. God gave us a wonderful gift of language. Words communicate our thoughts, feelings and ideas. Using words helps us to be connected to other people. But words can also hurt. You probably know what it's like to say something without thinking and hurt someone's feelings. You can't take back your words.

If you pull muddy water out of a well, you can try to clean the water with chemicals or a water purification system. But it's much easier just to have a clean well. While you might not be able to do anything about the dirt in a real well, you can do something about the dirt in the well of your heart. Fill your heart's well with God's Word and what comes up in your mouth's bucket will be clean and refreshing.

Receptionists for businesses are taught to smile when they answer the phone. Why do you think that's important? After all, no one can see you on the phone.

An author was worried about her first radio interview. The hostess doing the interview reminded her to smile. She said, "If you are smiling, people will hear your smile on the radio and respond well to you."

Remember when you speak to someone, whether on the phone, or in person, a smile wins out! Don't you feel good when someone smiles at you? What response do you have? Of course, you want to smile back. Listen to what God says about your smile.

Write Proverbs 15:13:

_____

_____

_____

_____

Your face reflects what is in your heart. As we learn more about the love of God, the words we speak to others will be more loving.

Write Proverbs 19:14:

_____

_____

_____

_____

God cares about the words that come out of your mouth! Sing some praise songs to yourself each morning. You will be surprised at the result. Or if you play an instrument, play music of praise to God. Choose music CDs that will help fill your heart and mind with God's Word.

Praising God brings joy to our hearts and to His as well. Sing praises with your friends. Look up Ephesians 5:19 and find out what the Apostle Paul said about singing.

_____

_____

_____

Now write 1 Thessalonians 4:18.

_____

_____

_____

_____

How wonderful is the gift of encouragement! The words, "Well done" can change someone's day. How do you feel when you hear "I'm praying for you today" from Mom as you leave for school and that big test, or "I'm thinking of you" from a friend when you are sick? That's encouragement!

Can you give an example of someone who encouraged your heart? What did that person do and say?

_____

_____

_____

_____

Can you give an example of a time you encouraged someone else? How can you encourage someone today?

_____

_____

_____

_____

God encourages us with His Word. Read Romans 15:4, 5. What is the purpose of what's written in the Scriptures?

_____

_____

_____

What does God give us through His Word?

_____

_____

_____

_____

In Psalm 119:103 says about God's Word, "How sweet are your words to my taste, sweeter than honey to my mouth!" Remember that others like to hear those sweet words from you as well.

> *I love you, Jesus.*
> *I love you, Mom.*
> *I love you, Dad.*
> *I love you, sister or brother*
> *I love you, friend.*

Perhaps you have been taught that if you can't say anything nice, don't say anything at all. Don't be a dry well! Practice giving compliments and saying things that encourage other people. Write some of your ideas here:

To your best friend:

_____

_____

_____

_____

To your teacher:

_____

_____

_____

To someone having a hard time with math:

_____

_____

_____

_____

To someone wearing a new outfit:

_____

_____

_____

_____

If you are encouraging someone with a compliment, be sure your compliment is sincere. What does Proverbs 26:28 say about flattery?

_____

_____

_____

_____

Because God is all truth, He expects us to be truthful. Jesus says He is the way, the truth and the life (John 14:6). We trust Jesus because He is truthful. Your friends will be drawn to you if you are truthful as well.

Has anyone ever spread a rumor about you? What did you do?

Have you ever been the one to spread a rumor about someone else? How did you feel about yourself?

Rumors snowball. Someone tells a bit of a story, the next person adds to it, and before long, a vicious, ugly story is out there. There may be just a hint of truth to it, but by now, it is just full of lies. In most cases, there is no truth.

Read Proverbs 18:6–8. Write in your own words what those verses mean.

_____

_____

_____

_____

We are responsible for the damage we do to someone's heart. A damaged reputation is not easy to repair. A heart that is tender to Jesus will not have any part in gossip. If you have no part in it, you will have a clean conscience.

Read Proverbs 12:17–19. What do you learn from this passage?

_____

_____

_____

_____

Remember, if you don't spread gossip, you are helping it to die. Proverbs 26:20 says, "Without wood a fire goes out; without gossip a quarrel dies down."

What terrific advice! The Bible gives good advice for real problems.

How do you need to change your words? Sometimes changing what you say starts with changing what you listen to. What do you do if someone tells a dirty story or joke? What *should* you do?

1 Thessalonians 5:22 says, "Avoid every kind of evil." Listening to dirty stories encourages the person telling the stories. Dirty stories dirty your heart. Learn to walk away.

Change your words so that you're using your mouth the way God wants you to use it. Write Ephesians 4:29 here.

_____

_____

_____

_____

We are to speak only words that build others up.

God also wants us to think carefully about what we say, and not to use certain language just because everyone else does. For example, God says that we should not misuse the name of the Lord (Exodus 20:7). That means that we should not use God's name in ways that we don't really mean or in ways that don't honor Him.

Philippians 2:9 tells us that Jesus' name is above every other name. We should speak His name to praise Him, and not to speak angrily at other people. Controlling the tongue is hard! But God helps us. What does Psalm 141:3 say?

_____

_____

_____

_____

How will God help you control your tongue?

_____

_____

_____

_____

We spend much of our time talking. If you are a child of the King, you represent the King everywhere you go and in every word you speak. Remember, knowing what the Word of God says is your best defense against the temptation to let muddy water come out of your heart's well.

In this lesson you've learned that God cares about what comes out of your mouth, and that what comes out of your mouth shows what is in your heart. You can use your mouth to share God's love and encourage others to know and trust him better.

You can learn more about how God wants you to use your mouth. Dig into Digging for Seeds of Faith on pages 80–81.

How will what you've learned help your faith in God to grow? In your journal, answer this question:

What seed of faith is planted in me today?

Remember that what you write in your journal is private and personal. You don't have to share it with anyone.

For the word of God is living and active.
Sharper than any double-edged sword, it penetrates
even to dividing soul and spirit,
joints and marrow;
it judges the thoughts and attitudes of the heart.

HEBREWS 4:12

PICTURES OF TRUTH

Read these two New Testament passages and answer the questions to learn more about what God says about honesty in what we say.

Acts 5:1–11 Ananias and Sapphira

What was in the hearts of Ananias and Sapphira?

_____

_____

_____

_____

What came out of the mouths of Ananias and Sapphira?

_____

_____

_____

_____

James 3:1–12 Taming the Tongue

List three "word pictures" you find in this passage about the tongue.

1. (verse 3)

_____

_____

_____

2. (verses 4, 5)

_____

_____

_____

3. (verses 6)

_____

_____

_____

Verse 12 tells us that:

A fig tree cannot bear olives.

A grapevine cannot bear figs.

A salt spring cannot produce fresh water.

Fill in this last example with your own words:

A _____ heart cannot produce _____ words.

How is My Heart?

The good man brings good things out of the goods stored up in
his heart, and the evil man brings evil things
out of the evil stored up in his heart.
For out of the overflow of his heart his mouth speaks.

LUKE 6:45

Remember the saying "What is down in the well comes up in the bucket?" from our last lesson? The things we think about, see, or hear are quickly transferred to our heart.

Write Matthew 6:21 here:

_____

_____

_____

_____

If you were going to look for a treasure, where would you look? Maybe thinking about treasure makes you think of adventure stories of hidden treasure or panning for gold in the Old West. When Jesus talked about treasure, He wanted us to think about what is important in our lives. Write down a few things that are important to you.

_____

_____

_____

_____

Our family and friends are treasures. All of us have a few favorite possessions. God wants us to enjoy these things because they are gifts from Him. When we forget that all the good things we have come from God, we start to store up the wrong kinds of treasures. That's when we start to think we don't have to depend on God any more.

What kind of heart does God want us to have. Look up Psalm 86:11 and write it here. Then underline the key word.

_____

_____

_____

God wants you to have an "undivided" heart. That means you show your love and loyalty to God in everything you do, because God has control of your heart. Then you don't have to worry about what God sees when He looks in your heart. Look up Psalm 139:23, 24 and read it. What does the psalmist ask God to do in these verses?

_____

_____

_____

What kinds of things might God find in someone's heart?

_____

_____

_____

What is the greatest thing you can have in your heart? God Himself! God sent Jesus into the world to be your Savior so that you could know

God and have a relationship with Him. When Jesus comes into your heart, He forgives your sins and you become a child of God. Does that mean you will never sin again? No. You'll always be tempted to sin, and many times you will choose the wrong thing, even though you know it's wrong. A close relationship with God will help you choose God's way more and more.

Write Psalm 119:11 here:

_____

_____

_____

_____

God gave us the Bible, His Word, so that we could know Him better and know how to please Him. When you read the Bible, you learn more about what God is like and how He wants you to live.

Do you have a friend who you spend time with every day? When you're together, you tell each other everything. When something sad happens, you both feel sad. When something great happens, you both celebrate. You know each other very well because you spend time together.

God wants that kind of friendship with you. Spend time with God every day. If you can, try to do it at the same time each day, and in the same place. Here are some ideas for spending time with God each day.

A Appreciate what God has done for you. Thank Him!

P Praise God for being God! No one else is like Him!

P Petition, or ask, God for the things that you need His guidance for.

L Listen to what God says. Read His Word and listen for His answers to your questions. Use a devotional book or Bible reading schedule to help you read God's Word.

E Expect that God will answer you and do something good in your life that day.

Start by spending 10 minutes alone with God each day. Establish a good habit, and you'll find your time growing to 15 or 20 minutes—or more. Then you'll be prepared to face your day and show the people around you what is in your heart.

Have you ever seen a rotten apple? You knew right away that it was rotten, didn't you. It didn't smell right. It didn't feel right when you held it in your hand. Hopefully you didn't bite into it! If the rotten apple were in a bowl with good apples, you would know right away which one to avoid.

Don't be the bad apple! You can't hide what's in your heart just by putting your good side forward. God knows what's in your heart, and others can see, too. For instance, what kind of friend are you?

Are you sincere?

Are you trustworthy?

Are you loyal?

Are you dependable?

If you are not sincere, your friends will know. If you can't be trusted, they will find out. They'll know if they can depend on you. What is in your heart will show in how you treat your friends. Use your words and actions to let other people know that Jesus is in your heart.

You are a child of the king! You show that in how you behave and also in how you appear to others. Read 1 Timothy 2:9, 10. Is it wrong to wear jewelry or nice clothes? Why or why not?

_____

_____

_____

_____

How does what you wear show what is important to you?

_____

_____

_____

Modesty, decency, and propriety are big words. But they all mean that we should make sure that the choices we make about our physical appearance are correct and proper so that we are pleasing not just to ourselves and others, but to God. If Jesus were coming to breakfast at your house, would that change how you decide to dress?

God knows that we will have "heart trouble." Some days you'll feel like nothing went right, or you'll be hurt by a friend. Some days you'll get angry at someone you love, or you won't have a moment's patience for anyone. God knows that those times will come, so He has given answers in His Word. If you've hidden His Word in your heart, the Holy Spirit will remind you of just the right verse to help.

Take a moment to pray and let God know your heart troubles. Ask Him to help you through so that you can show the world that Jesus is the treasure in your heart. You can use this prayer:

> Dear Lord, this is your child _____. Thank you for
> loving me. Fill my heart with your light, so that others around me
> will see you in me and bring glory to Your name. I need Your help,
> Lord. It is not always easy to do the right thing. Help me to
> depend on Your strength every day. Thank you, Father. Amen.

In this lesson you've learned that God wants you to store up His treasures in your heart. You learned some ideas for how to spend time with God and hide His Word in your heart. And you know that God gives answers to the troubles of your heart.

You can know more about how God wants you to store up treasures in your heart. Dig into Digging for Seeds of Faith on pages 89–91.

How will what you've learned help your faith in God to grow? In your journal, answer this question:

 What seed of faith is planted in me today?

Remember that what you write in your journal is private and personal. You don't have to share it with anyone.

✳ ❋ ✳

Even youths grow tired and weary and young men stumble and fall;
but those who hope in the Lord will renew their strength.
They will soar on wings like eagles;
they will run and not grow weary,
they will walk and not be faint.

ISAIAH 40: 30, 31

TREASURES OF THE HEART

What kinds of heart troubles keep you from showing the treasure in your heart? Read the verses listed below. Then match each one to the "heart trouble" that it can help solve.

Philippians 4:13   **Angry heart**

_____

_____

_____

_____

1 Thessalonians 5:16   **Discouraged heart**

_____

_____

_____

_____

James 1:19, 20   **Sad heart**

_____

_____

_____

John 14:1 Worried heart

_____

_____

_____

_____

How do your friends affect what is in your heart? Read each of these verses and then write down something that the verses teaches you about choosing your friends.

1 Corinthians 15:33

_____

_____

_____

_____

Proverbs 12:26

_____

_____

_____

_____

Proverbs 119:63
Psalm

_____

_____

_____

_____

_____

Romans 12:9

_____

_____

_____

_____

1 Samuel 16:7

_____

_____

_____

_____

Proverbs 22:1

_____

_____

_____

_____

* ❋ *

WHAT AM I HOLDING?

When I consider your heavens, the work of your fingers,
the moon and the stars, which you have set in place,
what is man that you are mindful of him,
the son of man that you care for him?

PSALM 8:3, 4

God who created the starry heavens—as the work of His fingers—
created your fingers. What an awesome God! Hands can be strong or
gentle. Fingers may be long and slender, or short and pudgy. Some
people have soft hands, others have callused hands. Your fingers bend
and squeeze and stretch to do hundreds of different things every day,
and you hardly notice. Imagine for a moment that you didn't have
hands. Many things would be a lot harder to do.

If you have ever injured your arm or hand, you have a special appreciation for your hands. Have you ever had your hand in a cast? It is
clumsy and really cramps your style!

We use our hands from the moment we hit the alarm button in the
morning until we climb back into bed at night. Throughout the day we
have eaten, written, played an instrument, dressed, groomed, petted an
animal and held the phone with our hands, just to mention a few things
Some of us even talk with our hands!

Our Heavenly Father cares what we do with our hands and arms.
He gave us strength for difficult tasks and tenderness to hold someone
dear. With the same hands we work and play, clap and pray.

Have you ever thought about the arms and hands of God? The Bible talks about the hands of God over and over again. Look up these verses and write something that you learned about the hand of God from each verse.

Psalm 18:35

_____

_____

_____

Psalm 20:6

_____

_____

_____

Psalm 37:24

_____

_____

_____

Psalm 95:4

_____

_____

_____

God uses His hands to show that He cares for you and that He is in control of the world that you live in. God created the world, and He still cares about what happens in the world. He cares what happens to you.

What about Jesus? What did He use his hands for while He lived on earth? Mark 10:13–16 tells us that Jesus used his hands to show that He cared for little children. People were bringing the children to Jesus to have Him touch them. His disciples thought the people were bothering Jesus too much and told the people to go away. But Jesus welcomed the little children. He took them in His arms, put His hands on them and blessed them. Jesus used His hands to give a blessing and let the children know that they were important to God.

You probably know a lot of the stories of how Jesus healed people. Have you ever noticed how much He used his hands? Here are a few passages to look up for some examples:

Matthew 8:1–3	Jesus heals a man with leprosy
Matthew 8:14, 15	Jesus heals Peter's mother-in-law
Mark 5:35–42	Jesus heals Jairus's daughter
John 9:1–11	Jesus heals a blind man

Jesus used His hands to show His compassion for people who needed His help. He could have healed without touching them, even without saying anything. But Jesus touched these people and they knew that He cared for them. Maybe you've had the experience of being upset or sad about something, and having someone's arms around you made you feel better. Imagine having Jesus' arms wrapped around you. His strong arms guide us through struggles. He holds us when we're afraid. He corrects us when we disobey.

Now think about the last week of Jesus' life. What is the last thing He did with His disciples before He was arrested and crucified? They had a meal together—the Last Supper. Jesus took the bread in His hands and broke it, saying, "This is my body, given for you" (Luke 22:19). He did the same thing with the cup. Jesus used His hands to give His followers—including us—a picture of how He gave His life for us.

Because Jesus gave His life for us, we can know God and have a relationship with Him. Because we have a relationship with God, He wants us to do the right things with our own hands. The first part of

Ecclesiastes 9:10 says, "Whatever your hand finds to do, do it with all your might." But what does God want our hands to find to do?

Look up Psalm143:5, 6 and write it here:

_____

_____

_____

_____

When you spread out your hands to God, you reach out for God the way you would reach for a drink if you were in a desert.

Read Psalm 47:1 and write it here:

_____

_____

_____

_____

What does this verse tell you to do with your hands? You can praise God in many different ways—including with your hands! You can clap your hands in worship or while singing a praise song, and that is praising God. You can also praise God with your hands by how you use them to serve other people.

Read Proverbs 14:31 and write it here:

_____

_____

_____

_____

You don't have to look very far to find someone who needs something, whether food, clothing, help with chores, tutoring in homework, or just someone to be a friend. When you reach out and touch someone with kindness, you honor God. The more you think about God's kindness to you, the more you will want to show kindness to other people.

Make a short list of ways you can show kindness by doing things with your hands.

_____

_____

_____

_____

Pete was a kindhearted young man who noticed that another boy at school was always alone. Pete decided to show acts of kindness by slipping anonymous notes and McDonald's coupons in the other boy's desk. He enjoyed watching the boy open his desk and find surprises. After a while, the boy left the school and Pete didn't see him any more.

A couple of years later, Pete and his buddies were walking downtown. Another group of guys came up and started fighting with them. Pete recognized one of them—the boy he had given coupons to. The boy was in a gang now. Pete looked him right in the eye and said, "I'm the friend who gave you those cards." Immediately the other boy said, "Stop! Nobody is going to hurt my friend."

You never know when acts of kindness will come back to you. Learning to serve others is one of the most rewarding lessons you can learn. Think of a neighbor who needs help with her weeding, or bake cookies for someone you know who might be lonely. Help a busy mom with her baby, or volunteer at church or the hospital.

Your willing hands and joyful spirit can make others want to know Jesus better. Ephesians 6:7 says, "Serve wholeheartedly, as if you were serving the Lord, not men, because you know that the Lord will reward everyone for whatever good he does." Some of your greatest memories will be about times you helped someone else, whether you got any recognition or not. Reach out your hands and arms to others this week. Ask God to show you someone in need, then reach out and touch somebody.

Keep your hands pure. Be careful what you pick up and hold. Be careful what you use your hands to do. Fold your hands in prayer and pray something like this:

> Heavenly Father, You are awesome. You made my hands. Help me to praise you with my hands. Please keep my hands and heart pure. Don't let me give into temptation to use my hands to do things that I know are wrong. I ask for strong arms to face struggles and gentle hands to help the hurting. Thank you for holding me in Your arms and sheltering me under Your wings. Amen.

In this lesson you've learned that Jesus used His hands to bless and minister to other people. You've seen how God wants you to use your hands to praise Him and to serve Him. You've thought about things you can do with your Hands to show kindness to others and help them know God better because of what you do.

If you want to know more about how God wants you to serve Him with your hands, turn to Digging for Seeds of Faith on pages 97–99.

How will what you've learned help your faith in God to grow? In your journal, answer this question:

 What seed of faith is planted in me today?

Remember that what you write in your journal is private and personal. You don't have to share it with anyone.

Teach me to do your will, for you are my God.
May your good Spirit lead me on level ground.
PROVERBS 143:10

✳ ❉ ✳

HANDS TO HELP AND HANDS TO HOLD

Hands to help and hands to hold,
Hands to raise and hands to fold.
Hands to carry other's burdens,
Hands to ease a heavy load.
Gentle hands, a gentle touch,
Strong hands show "I care so much."
Old hands, gnarled, wise and knowing,
Young hands, not a wrinkle showing.
Hands at work and hands at play,
Giving thanks to God today.
Reach your hand to touch another,
Mother, father, sister, brother.
Friends you love and friends to be,
May they see Your love in me!

BETTY HUIZENGA, © 2002

Psalm 24:3, 4 says, "Who may ascend the hill of the Lord? Who may stand in his holy place? He who has clean hands and a pure heart."

Just as you want to protect your hands from injury, also keep your hands from sinning. Your hands are busy all day long. Sometimes the mind works so fast the hands don't keep up. It's easy to make a gesture with your hands or pick up something that doesn't honor God. A split-second later, you realize you should not have done that.

God knits our hands and hearts together. He brings together every part of you—mind, eyes, ears, mouth, heart, hands, and feet—to make you the person you are so that you can serve Him.

Give an example of using your hands to serve God in these situations:

· Studying for a test

_____

_____

_____

_____

· Helping around the house

_____

_____

_____

_____

· Volunteering at church

_____

_____

_____

_____

· Encouraging someone

_____

_____

_____

_____

· Doing the right thing when it's hard

_____

_____

_____

_____

·   **Making right something that you did wrong**

_____

_____

_____

_____

Whatever you do, work at it with all your heart, as working for the Lord, not for men, since you know that you will receive an inheritance from the Lord as a reward. It is the Lord Christ you are serving (Colossians 3:23).

* ✳ *

WHERE AM I GOING?

He has showed you, O man, what is good.
And what does the Lord require of you?
To act justly and to love mercy
and to walk humbly with your God.

MICAH 6:8

Athletes train for years to compete at the Olympic Games. Many athletes think of the Olympics as the most important competition to be in. They sacrifice time and money to train with the best coaches, just so they can be ready for an event that happens only once every four years. But you can learn a lot from what an Olympic champion goes through. You might not compete in the Olympics, but you are running a race.

The Bible uses the picture of an athlete running a race to teach us about how God wants us to live our lives. 1 Corinthians 9:24, 25 says, "Do you not know that in a race all the runners run, but only one gets the prize? Everyone who competes in the games goes into strict training. They do it to get a crown that will not last; but we do it to get a crown that will last forever."

Champion athletes get a prize that lasts until someone else runs faster or jumps higher. But the reward that God gives lasts forever. How does God want us to train for the race of life? Read Proverbs 4:25–27 and write one idea from each sentence.

1.

Listen to God's Word

2.

Keep God's Word in sight + heart

3.

Guard your heart = Love God

4. _Try to live a righteous life_

In the Winter 2002 Olympics, a speed skating race had a surprising ending. One man finished the race and began his victory lap. Right behind him another man began a victory lap. What happened? It turned out that the first man had broken a rule and bumped the second man, so he was disqualified. The second man was the true winner. You can't win if you don't follow the rules. The Bible says something just like that.

Write 2 Timothy 2:5 here:

If anyone competes as an athlete he does not achieve the victors co... unless he compete according to the rules

What does this verse tell you about running life's race?

It is best to follow good advice + rules

_____

_____

Running a race is difficult. You can get out of breath, or get a pain in your side—ouch! You can become discouraged when others run ahead of you. You may even be tempted to quit.

Sometimes the race of life is difficult as well. Sometimes we are discouraged. We may be too busy and become tired and weak. We can feel like we have failed when others seem to succeed. You can overcome some of those feelings by being prepared for the race.

Write Philippians 3:13, 14:

Do not look back with regrets but look ahead to what God has called you (us) to be

According to this verse, what do we need to do to win the race?

hope, trust in God that we are forgiven and trust that God gives what you need to succeed.

Paul talks about highest prize people before him Jesus he knows persevered X ins

Now is the time to start preparing for the race of life. The more you learn to follow Jesus now, the better equipped you will be for every situation that comes up along the road. You'll run into roadblocks and ruts in the road, there will be temptations that try to sidetrack you. You may even stumble occasionally, but God will pick you up and help you to continue. Psalm 37:23–25 says, "If the Lord delights in a man's way, he makes his steps firm; though he stumble, he will not fall, for the Lord upholds him with his hand."

In the *Appleseeds* lessons you've learned how important it is to stand for Jesus, no matter where, no matter when, no matter who else is there. Matters that are settled in your heart will keep your feet on the right path. You'll always have just the right map to help you find your way.

Read Matthew 7:13, 14. Describe the two roads.

Narrow path

broad road

What sometimes makes it hard to choose the right road?

- world we live in

- friends - peer pressure

- sometimes narrow is harder

If someone tempts you, have your answer decided and ready in your heart. What do you say when someone offers alcohol, cigarettes or drugs to you? What if a person tempts you with impurity of any kind? Do you have a steady, ready answer? God gives you His protection for the tough times. Look up Ephesians 6:14–18 and write a list of what God gives you to put on. *Armour of God*

belt of truth   *helmet of salvation*

breastplate of righteousness

feet - readiness   *Sword of the spirit*

shield of faith   *Prayer*

This passage talks about top to toe protection. God doesn't leave any part of you unprotected. Notice especially what He gives you for your feet—readiness that comes from the gospel of peace. He'll make you ready for whatever situation you face, so that you can spread the good news about Jesus by what you do and say.

God also gives you people to help you run the race. Read these verses and write down the kind of person God gives you.

Proverbs 13:20

Wise people _vs_ _fool._
_____
_____
_____

Proverbs 18:24

Good friends
_____
_____
_____

Ephesians 6:1–3

Parents
_____
_____

Berg+s   ask adults older friendship —

Friendship is one of the great blessings of life. It may be hard for you to imagine now, but some of the friends you have now may be you friends for your whole life. Choose wisely!

It's normal to have some disagreements with your parents as you grow up. What God wants you to do is honor and respect them. If they know Jesus, they want to show you God's way.

In the *Appleseeds* classes you've met mentors and other adults who care about how you learn to walk in God's ways. Don't forget that they can give you wise advice. Believe it or not, they may have gone through just what you're going through.

We all know the comfort of holding the hand of someone we trust. We feel safe and ever so loved. Next time you feel alone, close your eyes and imagine Jesus walking right beside you, holding your hand. He is! Pray a prayer like this one to let God know you're glad He's with you.

> Precious Heavenly Father, thank you for creating me. Thank you
> for a good mind, my eyesight and my hearing. Keep my tongue
> from evil, and guard my heart. Hold my hand and help me to use
> them in service to others. Lead me on the straight path that leads
> to happiness and fulfillment. You are the King of Kings, and I
> praise Your holy name. In Jesus' name I pray. Amen.

In this lesson you've learned that God has a race for you to run, and
you can win the race! Better yet, God gives you everything you need
to run the race, from training advice to equipment. You've seen that by
running the race well, you can spread the gospel of peace.

Learn more about how God wants you to serve Him with your feet,
turn to Digging for Seeds of Faith on pages 106–107.

How will what you've learned help your faith in God to grow? In
your journal, answer this question:

 What seed of faith is planted in me today?

Remember that what you write in your journal is private and
personal. You don't have to share it with anyone.

> *Be strong and courageous. Do not be afraid or terrified*
> *because of them, for the Lord your God goes with you;*
> *he will never leave you nor forsake you.*
> **DEUTERONOMY 31:7**

RUN WITH GOD

The Bible gives lots of help for how to run the race of life and win! No human coach could do a better job of helping you train for the big race. Look up each of these verses. Then write down what training tip you find in that verse to help you run the race God has given you.

Psalm 119:32

I run in th paths of your commands for you have set me free

Isaiah 30:21

Whethr you turn ti left or right you will hear a voice behind you saying "This is the way walk in take it

Proverbs 3:5-6

love & faithfulness / Trust God and acknowledge God in your life

Hebrews 12:1

clouds of witnesses

Isaiah 40:31

hope — soar as eagles

Psalm 119:105

Your word is a lamp unto
my feet

Proverbs 4:11, 12

God's guidance is there

Psalm 121:3

God watches over
to protect you

Who Is God?

Step 1: Life Craft

Gather scrapbooking supplies that girls can use to create personal journals to use throughout the *Appleseeds* classes. You can use craft papers, bright card stock or wallpaper samples for covers. Use colored paper or craft papers for the inside pages. Punch holes down one side and tie the journal together with pretty ribbon or jute. Decorate the covers with glitter glue, markers or gel pens.

As girls arrive, invite them to begin making a journal. Encourage the girls to use individual creativity given by God to make their private journals. As they work, talk about the "Children of the King" theme of *Appleseeds* and encourage the girls to find creative ways to represent this idea on the cover of their journals.

Keep a camera handy and take photos of the crafts in progress each week. Girls will enjoy including these in their journals. Take a photograph of your class the first week. Make a copy for each girl and present it the following week for girls to add to their journals.

Make a class list of names and phone numbers, so the girls can contact one another. Be sure to include the names of the mentors on the sheet. Tell the girls that they are welcome to call you to talk about the lesson or anything else that is on their minds.

It is important that each girl feels secure and knows that everything she shares will be kept in strictest confidence. As your group gets to know each other, some girls may share very personal information because they trust everyone there. Let girls know how important it is to keep in confidence the things that other girls share. Being trustworthy is part of being a good Christian friend.

Step 2. Bible Study Tips

Because this is the first lesson, girls may be receiving their books for the first time when you meet. As you go through the lesson, invite girls who are comfortable reading aloud to take turns. Keep the atmosphere comfortable for everyone by not forcing someone to read if she's not confident.

As girls look up Bible verses, give them hints about where they might find the right book of the Bible: "in the Old Testament"; "near the front of the Bible"; "the last book of the Bible" and so on. Give girls who don't know their way around the Bible plenty of time to find the passage and copy the verse.

Depending on the time you have, you might work through the Digging for Seeds of Faith pages as a group, or ask girls to work in small groups to find the answers. Then review them together. If your time is limited, draw the girls' attention to this activity and challenge them to complete it before you meet again.

· ·

What is God Like? ANSWERS

Matthew 5:48	God is perfect.
Psalm 139:7–12	God is everywhere.
Ezekiel 11:5	God knows everything.
Psalm 145:9	God is good.
Psalm 111:7	God is just.
1John 2:1	God is righteous.
Daniel 9:9	God is merciful.

· ·

Step 3. Manners Matter

Good manners reflect personality and character. If girls practice good manners, they'll be less likely to feel embarrassed in public, in a new situation, when they meet someone new, or when they eat at a beautiful restaurant. When they know the right thing to do, they'll be more confident. A girl who is self-confident can concentrate on others, not just herself.

In this first lesson, practice making introductions. Some of the girls may not know each other very well. Begin by reviewing some basics, such as:

- Shake hands confidently.
- When you meet someone new, look the person in the eye.
- Stand up straight.
- When you introduce two friends to each other, make sure to say their names clearly.
- Repeat the name of the person you've met: "I'm glad to meet you, Jane."
- Introduce yourself to someone new in a friendly way.

Then choose trios of girls, suggest a situation, and ask them to make introductions. Some situations might be: introducing two friends at school to each other; introducing yourself to a visitor at church; introducing a friend to a parent for the first time; introducing a parent to a teacher; introducing a younger person to an older person.

Step 4. Wrapping Up

Take time to pray for the girls and mention each one by name. Close by singing a familiar song or chorus about the awesomeness of God.

How Can I Know God?

Step 1: Life Craft

Gather these supplies: construction paper, pencils, ruler, scissors, small paint brushes, white glue, pressed or dried flowers or leaves, clear self-adhesive plastic with peel-off backing. The girls will use these supplies to create bookmarks to remind them that they are precious to God and He wants them to know Him through His Word. When they're finished, encourage the girls to keep the bookmarks in their Bibles.

Girls can cut the construction paper to the size they like. Then have them lay the pressed or dried flowers on the paper in any pattern they like. If anyone is using a large piece of flower, it's a good idea to brush a little glue on the back before placing it. Then cut a piece of self-adhesive plastic slightly larger than the construction paper shape. Peel off the backing and place the plastic over the shape. Press firmly against the design. Trim the edges.

Step 2. Bible Study Tips

Walk through the lesson pages together, pausing to read the verses and share reflections. Be ready with examples from your own life. Remind the girls they can use their bookmarks to mark favorite verses. You can enrich your discussion with these ideas:

- Read Psalm 51:1–7 together as you talk about our sin and God's forgiveness.
- Look up these additional verses: Hebrews 13:5-6; Psalm 119:9–11.
- Talk about the "Golden Rule" and how we reflect God's forgiveness when we forgive others.

As you come to the end of the lesson, focus on the concept of knowing God and becoming His child. If you know that some of the girls have already committed their lives to Christ, invite one or two to share with the group about that decision. Be sure to ask ahead of time so that no one feels put on the spot.

If the Apostles Creed is important in your church tradition, go through Digging for Seeds of Faith together.

. . . .

Apostles' Creed ANSWERS

I believe in God, the Father, Almighty, Maker of heaven and earth,
> *God, who made the universe, is our Father.*

and in Jesus Christ, His only begotten Son, our Lord, who was conceived by the Holy Spirit, born of the virgin Mary,
> *Jesus is God because He came from the Holy Spirit, not a human father. When Jesus came into the world, God Himself came into the world as a human.*

suffered under Pontius Pilate, was crucified, dead and buried. He descended into hell. The third day, He arose again from the dead.
> *Jesus, a real human who lived in history, died a real death. But God raised him up again.*

He ascended into heaven and is seated at the right hand of God the Father.
> *Jesus went to heaven, where He came from. He reigns with his Father.*

From there He will come to judge the living and the dead.
> *Someday Jesus will come back to earth. He will judge everyone with God's judgment.*

I believe in the Holy Spirit,
> *The Holy Spirit is God Himself, and He's active in believers.*

the holy catholic church,
> *Everyone who has faith in Jesus is part of one body of believers all over the world.*

the forgiveness of sins,
> *God really does forgive our sins! We don't earn forgiveness; God gives it freely.*

the communion of the Saints,
> *Everyone who has faith in Jesus is a saint, and the example of other saints, whether living or not, can help us live the Christian life.*

the resurrection of the body, and life everlasting.
> *When Jesus comes back to reign, He will raise us also. We'll have new bodies and live forever with him.*

. . . .

Step 3: Manners Matter

Getting to know someone new can be awkward for some girls. Give them some quick tips for making conversation with someone they don't know well:

- Ask questions that encourage the other person to talk, but don't ask nosy questions. Nod or smile to show you're paying attention.
- Don't interrupt.
- If someone asks you a question, say more than "yes" or "no." Don't mumble.
- When the conversation seems to be ending, say "It was nice to talk with you."

Now let the girls practice by acting out these situations: meeting someone at a party; welcoming a visitor at church; making friends with someone new at school; talking to someone whose name you don't remember; talking to an adult at a fancy dinner. Use a stop watch or second hand to give pairs of girls two minutes to begin a conversation and keep it going.

Step 4: Wrapping Up

Close your time together by thanking God for making a way for us to be His children. If the girls are comfortable, invite them to pray for each other. Sing "I Submit, O Father." You'll find the music on page 139.

> I submit, O Father, to Your will and way,
> And I treasure every word that You say.
> Help me to understand Your wisdom and Your plan,
> And keep me knitted in the palm of Your hand.

BETTY HUIZENGA, © 1999

Who Am I?

Step 1: Life Craft

This project takes some planning ahead. Gather enough muslin or strong plain cloth to trace the length of all the girls in your group. About four yards per girl is a good rule of thumb. Strips of colorful calico will also work. To save time, cut the fabric into lengths and pin two layers together. Arrange for several women with sewing machines to be on hand for this session. You'll need a lot of polyester batting for the end of class. To share expense, you might prefer to ask each girl to bring her own supplies, such as a bed sheet for the fabric and bags of stuffing.

As each girl arrives, have her lie down on top of doubled muslin. Trace around the entire girl. Use a "mitten" shape around hands and feet. Let girls cut out their own shapes, but make sure the cutting is well-supervised to make sure everything comes out evenly and well shaped. You might want to use a cardboard template for the head shape. Then invite the girls to move on with you to the Bible study portion of your time. Meanwhile, get your helpers going with their sewing machines! Stitch the cloth around the edges and then turn the shapes inside out.

Step 2: Bible Study Tips

Invite a knitter to come to this class. At the beginning of class, ask her to show a ball of yarn and some needles. Show how to start the stitches, then while the lesson is going on, she will just knit.

Take a few minutes to talk about the girls' visions of a throne room. Consider having newsprint and art supplies available and let girls work together in small groups to make an artistic presentation of what they imagine.

Psalm 139 is full of word pictures: going out and lying down (v.3); being hemmed in (v. 5); going up to the heavens (v. 8); bed in the depths (v. 8); wings of the dawn (v. 9); far side of the sea (v. 9); woven together in the depths of the earth (v. 15). Some girls will be drawn to the beauty of the language. Take time to hear their impressions of these words.

As you move through Psalm 139 and talk about how lovingly and uniquely God has created each of us, invite the girls to share something about their family heritages. What nationalities do their families represent? Do any speak another language? Do they have favorite foods in their families? Do their families have special traditions? We celebrate the families and heritages that God has given us. But no matter how much we are like others, we are not *exactly* like anyone else. Each of us is unique.

Take some time to pause on the topic of prayer, emphasizing the privilege of bringing our concerns to the King of Kings. Use the Digging for Seeds of Faith section as a guide to talk about the elements of prayer.

Ask your "knitter" to show what she has done during the lesson and talk about how the yarn has become something lovely and strong.

. . . .

Approaching the Throne ANSWERS

There are no right or wrong answers to this section. Encourage the girls to share what they've written down about prayer. Add some of your own ideas.

. . . .

Step 3: Manners Matters

How does a child of God dress? Modesty—a physical appearance that does not draw inappropriate attention—is part of good manners. Help girls understand that when they dress immodestly or inappropriately, others around them may feel uncomfortable. A child of God sets the example of being well-dressed, neat and clean in clothes that are appropriate to the situation.

Dressing appropriately:

- Shows honor and respect to God;
- Shows respect for others;
- Shows awareness of the feelings of others;
- Makes others comfortable so we can share God's love with them.

On slips of paper, write some situations that may require decisions about appropriate dress. Put these in a bowl or hat. Have girls pull them out one at a time and talk about appropriate dress for that situation. Encourage the girls to explain why they think what they think. Some possible situations: the beach; dress-down day at school; church; dinner in a fancy restaurant; a very hot summer day; a concert. If you wish, you could gather a variety of clothing to use as props in talking about these situations.

Step 4: Wrapping Up

Reunite the girls with their stitched-up full-size dolls. Have each girl draw her face on with permanent markers (use pencil first). Stuff with polyester batting and stitched closed. Each girl will take her personalized doll home and dress it in some of her clothes that represent her image. If you need to save time, send the empty dolls and stuffing home separately for girls to finish at home. Close with a prayer.

What Am I Thinking?

Step 1: Life Craft

Visit a hobby shop and gather some supplies that the girls can use to make "garlands of grace." Depending on the time of year, you might want to use evergreen or fresh cut flowers and florist wire. You can also use tiny silk flowers twisted together or shells and beads strung on ribbons. This is an opportunity for the girls to create something that they think is beautiful, something that they would be proud to wear or hang in their rooms. As you work, talk informally about what kinds of jewelry or accessories they like to wear and why.

Step 2: Bible Study Tips

The "garlands of grace" that the girls made as they arrived expressed their individuality. No two garlands will be alike, any more than any two girls are exactly alike. Point out that they were able to use their creativity to create the garlands because of the minds that God gave them. What makes one person pick up a yellow flower and another person choose the red one?

Our minds get information through our senses—through the things we see, hear, touch and smell. The brain has a powerful capacity to store this information. Even when we think we've long forgotten something, the memory is permanently stored in our brains. What we think and feel is influenced even by things that we don't remember experiencing.

Walk through the lesson pages together, pausing to read the verses and share reflections. As you talk about Romans 12:2, pause on the topic of "patterns of this world." Ask the girls to tell you patterns they conform to. How often do they choose to conform to what's happening around them, and how often does it happen before they've even realized it?

Challenge the girls to think about whether it's possible to choose what we think about. Can we really control our thoughts? After some discussion, make the point that we can choose what we expose ourselves to. Much of the time we can choose what we look at, what we listen to and so on. These experiences form memories and patterns of thinking in our minds.

We can't choose everything that happens to us. But when we can choose, God helps us make choices of integrity—choices that show that we belong to Him and want Him to transform us. Use the Digging for Seeds of Faith section to talk more about choices that please God.

"Not to decide is to decide." The challenge is to make intentional choices, not accidental ones, about the experiences that make us who we are—and who God wants us to be.

. . . .

Choices That Please God ANSWERS

Ephesians 6:1	God wants me to choose to *obedient*.
Proverbs 1:8, 9	God wants me to choose to *listen to my parents*.
Hebrews 12:14	God wants me to choose to *live in peace*.
Ephesians 4:32	God wants me to choose to *be kind, compassionate and forgiving*.
Psalm 37:4	God wants me to choose to *find delight in the Lord*.
1 Thessalonians 5:18	God wants me to choose to *be thankful at all times*.
Proverbs 3:5, 6	God wants me to choose to *trust in the Lord*.
John 14:23	God wants me to choose to *love Jesus and obey his teaching*.

. . . .

Step 3: Manners Matter

God gave us a great gift of salvation! And we're thankful. Help the girls understand that they can show the "mind of Christ" to other people when they show their appreciation. Provide a selection of tasteful thank-you cards or blank notes. If possible, gather some fun gel pens or other kinds of pens the girls would enjoy using.

Talk about the key parts of a thank-you note, such as using the person's name, sounding sincere, being specific about what you're thankful for, writing neatly and being prompt with notes. Talk about some occasions when it is appropriate to write notes, such as thanking a teacher who has helped with a special project; thanking a friend's mom for having you over to dinner; thanking people for birthday or holiday gifts. Ask the girls to think of a person they'd like to express thanks or appreciation to as a way of sharing the mind of Christ. Play some praise and worship music and give girls time to write the notes. You might want to provide stamps for girls who would like to mail their notes.

Step 4: Wrapping Up

Ask the girls to take another look at the "garlands of grace" that they made earlier. Challenge them to use the garlands as reminders to keep their minds focused on Jesus, whether they wear them or hang them as a decoration. Close by singing a song about staying focused on pleasing God.

What Am I Looking At?

Step 1. Life Craft

Purchase small mirrors with borders at a craft or hobby store. The borders may be cardboard, unfinished pressed board or plastic. Gather some decorating supplies, or ask the girls to bring items that show their individual interests, such as photos, flowers, beads, buttons, ribbons, and bows. Use craft glue or rubber cement to affix the items to the border of the mirror. Use this craft time to talk informally about things that are beautiful to look at. Find out what the girls enjoy. Make sure that at least one mentor has a conversation with each girl.

Step 2. Bible Study Tips

Find out how many of the girls have completed the study ahead of time. Adapt the depth of your discussion to how prepared the girls are and what you already know about their spiritual experience.

Ask the girls to bring their decorated mirrors to the Bible study portion of your time. Stir up the gigglies in the girls by asking them to make silly expressions with their faces, especially their eyes. Set an example with a few of your own! Have the girls look in the mirrors and see their own faces.

Remind the girls that they used their eyes to be expressive, to look at others' expressions, and to see their own expressions. Our eyes are a gift from God. We see the world through our eyes, and we use our eyes to share ourselves with the world. Light reflecting in the mirror helped the girls to see themselves. God's Word is a mirror that reflects God's light into the eyes of our hearts.

Walk through the lesson pages together, pausing to read the verses and share reflections. Ask the girls to share some specific situations where they needed God's light on their paths in order to know what to do. Perhaps they have favorite Bible verses to share.

If it's possible, darken the room at this point. Shine flashlights into the mirrors and watch how the light spreads all around the room. Use this as a picture of how we are shining stars for Jesus. We make choices for how to use our eyes every day. Challenge the girls to make choices that will help them be shining stars reflecting the light of Jesus to others who need to see it. Use the Digging for Seeds of Faith section to talk more about what God wants us to see with our eyes.

. . . .

Eyes of the Heart ANSWERS

God wants me to use my eyes...

Psalm 19:8	To see God's commands.
Psalm 25:15	To keep my eyes on the Lord.
Psalm 118:23	To see the marvelous things God has done.
Psalm 141:8	To keep my eyes fixed on the Lord.
Proverbs 17:24	To keep wisdom in view.
Psalm 121:1	To lift my eyes to God for help.
Ephesians 1:18	To see the hope that He calls me to.

. . . .

Step 3. Manners Matter

The girls you're teaching are on the verge of adolescence—and a lot of changes! While you don't want to teach that physical appearance is more important than what's on the inside, it's good to remember that many girls are self-conscious about how they look. They know that other people are looking at them. How they feel about their appearance may affect how they feel about themselves. So whether you have a class full of raving natural beauties or a band of ragamuffins, take some time to help the girls feel good about how they look. Depending on the girls' interests and the talents of your mentors and moms, you can choose from a variety of activities:

- Someone clever with hair styles could share some tips for fixing hair.
- Older girls in the group may be experimenting with make-up and would appreciate some tips.
- Ask a seamstress to demonstrate some basic mending or decorative techniques that will revitalize favorite clothing.
- Invite someone to help girls discover which colors of clothing are flattering to their complexions.
- Bring in an assortment of blouses, vests, sweaters and jackets. Put on an impromptu modeling show. Talk about what looks good together and why.

Step 4. Wrapping Up

Ask the girls to take one last look in their mirrors and remind them that God is looking at their hearts. Close by singing a song that asks God to open our eyes to see Him and follow His way. Take time to pray for each girl, asking God to help the girls see His light this week.

What Am I Listening To?

Step 1: Life Craft

For this project, plan ahead and ask the girls each to bring an unfrosted cake to the session. If you know someone who is talented at cake decorating techniques, invite her as a special guest. If not, you can still make this time challenging and interesting to the girls.

Gather the ingredients for making frosting. You can use any favorite recipe you like. Set up several "stations" with supplies the girls need. Depending on the size of your group and how much space you have, you may want the girls to work in groups of two to four. Make sure you have the girls' attention and explain that you are going to give oral instructions for making frosting and decorating their cakes. They have to listen carefully to know what to do. Do not repeat your instructions; make it essential that they listen to you!

If you have a cake decorator special guest, you may prefer to prepare or buy frosting ahead of time and focus on having the girls listen to decorating instructions.

Step 2: Bible Study Tips

Use an assortment of noisemakers and see how the girls respond. You might blow a whistle, bang a pot with a wooden spoon, play a chord on a piano or start singing a silly song. Their heads will turn. They may think you a little strange for the moment, but they'll be paying attention!

Give the girls an opportunity to talk about what makes it hard to pay attention sometimes—at school, to their parents, to their other responsibilities. As you go through the verses about listening to God and paying attention to his teachings, look for opportunities to share specific times in your life when you either listened or disobeyed God or your parents. Share the consequences with the girls. Invite the girls to share similar stories.

Walk through the lesson pages together. Emphasize that paying attention to God leads to making wise choices about what else we listen to, including music, family, radio programs, friends' advice and so on.

When you talk about the benefits of memorizing Scripture, be sure to give the girls an opportunity to recite verses that they have learned. Some of them will have been learning verses since they were very small. Let them share some of their favorites or some they learned a long time ago. Then talk about how the words have stuck with them. Invite them to share what the verses mean to them now.

Use the Digging for Seeds of Faith section to talk more about who God wants us to listen to. Underscore that God listens to the girls! He wants to share His wisdom with them because He cares about them. When they listen to God, He speaks, and when they talk to Him, He cares.

· ·

Ears of the Heart A N S W E R S

God wants me to pay attention because...

Proverbs 1:8	My parents have something to teach me.
Proverbs 8:32-33	God's instruction is wise.
Jeremiah 29:11	God has a plan for me.
Ephesians 5:21	I can show reverence for Christ.
James 3:17-18	Wisdom comes from heaven.

· ·

Step 3: Manners Matter
Group girls in pairs. Ask each girl to share something about herself with her partner. Tell them to be specific and tell the entire story. Then have the partner tell her story. At the end of ten minutes, blow a loud whistle or noisemaker. That will get everyone's attention! Have the girls share the story they heard and see how well they were listening. Let the person who told the story be the final judge and give a score from 1 (not listening at all) to 5 (listened very well) and explain the score.

Step 4: Wrapping Up
Close by singing "Loving Your Children." The music for this song is on page 140. Other songs are available on the website www.applesofgold.org. Or, recite the words (printed on the next page) as a prayer of blessing over the girls. Invite mentors to place their hands on the girls as you prayerfully recite the words. End with big hugs all around!

Bless the children, Lord.
Fill them with your goodness.
May their hearts and minds be ever fixed on you.
May their eyes see only
Things both pure and lovely,
And their ears hear only what you want them to.
May their lips speak only
Things both kind and true,
But speak boldly when they tell their love for you.
May their hands be gentle,
And their arms be strong,
Reaching out to others as they live each day.
May they run with boldness
The race you set before them.
Keep their feet forever on the narrow way.

BETTY HUIZENGA, © 1999

What Am I Saying?

Step 1: Life Craft

You'll need a new toothbrush for each girl, craft glue, and an assortment of decorative items, such as tiny silk flowers, sequins, beads, small shells, ribbons, and glitter glue pens. As girls arrive, invite them to decorate the tooth brushes in any way they'd like. They can add items down the back of the handle in a creative design and tie ribbon streamers around the bottom. They'll know that you plan to talk about the mouth! This toothbrush will be a visual reminder of the lesson. Let them know that they don't actually have to use it, so they can be as creative as they like. If you wish, you could also provide supplies for them to paint or decorate cups or mugs to use as toothbrush holders. Set the projects aside to dry during the Bible study time.

Step 2: Bible Study Tips

You might find that as they work on their decorative toothbrushes, girls will naturally begin telling each other stories that involve their mouths in some way. Listen in! You might hear something you can use an example in the lesson. Be ready with some examples from your own life about how we use our mouths to communicate, build relationships and show what is important to each of us.

Bring in two buckets filled with water. Make sure one bucket is clean and the water safe to drink. Fill the other bucket with dirty water. Without revealing the water, dip a cup in the clean bucket and offer a drink to one of the girls. Ask if anyone else wants a drink. Dip a cup in the dirty bucket and offer it to another girl. They'll get the point!

Walk through the lesson together, pausing to look up verses and to share reflections. Whenever you can, use examples of what you've heard the girls say to each other as positive models for speaking encouraging words.

The lesson includes a section for the girls to write down ideas for how to speak encouragingly to other people. Ask them to share some of their ideas. Then suggest the situations below and ask them for ideas about what to say. Do as many as you have time for. Depending on the size of your group, you might want to have them pair up and act them out.

- A younger sibling learns to do something new.
- A friend gets angry and says something insulting.
- Mom or Dad tries a new recipe for dinner.
- A friend at school is sick and misses a lot of classes.
- Someone starts a rumor that may or may not be true.

Use Digging for Seeds of Faith to talk more about using the tongue to honor God.

. . . .

Pictures of Truth A N S W E R S

Acts 5:1–11 Ananias and Sapphira
What was in the hearts of Ananias and Sapphira? (Greed. Satan.)
What came out of the mouths of Ananias and Sapphira? (They lied about how much money they had.)

James 3:1–12 Taming the Tongue
List three "word pictures" you find in this passage about the tongue.

1. (verse 3) A bit in a horse's mouth.
2. (verses 4, 5) The rudder of a ship.
3. (verses 6) A fire.

Verse 12 tells us that:
A fig tree cannot bear olives.
A grapevine cannot bear figs.
A salt spring cannot produce fresh water.

Fill in this last example with your own words:

A _____ heart cannot produce _____ words.
Girls will fill in the metaphor many different ways. Let them share.
. . . .

Step 3: Manners Matter
A word of affirmation can turn around someone's bad day! Girls in this age bracket know what it feels like to be teased or made fun of. Sometimes kids

say insulting things about other kids to make themselves look better. Encourage the girls to look for ways to speak positively and build each other up.

Ask the girls to share some of the best compliments they've ever received. They may be shy about this at first, but encourage them to speak out. Talk about why compliments make people feel better, then give several compliments to the girls as a group. Now toss a small ball or beanbag to one of the girls. The girl who catches it gives a compliment to someone else in the group, then tosses the ball to another girl.

Step 4: Wrapping Up
Let the girls get their decorated toothbrushes, which should be dry by now. Ask the girls to brainstorm phrases that express what they've learned from the lesson. Together, choose the best three. Encourage the girls to write these in their journals. Pray together, asking God to guard the mouths of everyone in the group. Close your time together by singing a favorite song about using lips or mouths to praise God.

What's in My Heart?

Step 1: Life Craft

Decorate small Blessing Boxes. You can use heart-shaped boxes or you can decorate a square or rectangular box with heart shapes or stickers. Craft and hobby stores have a large selection of interesting boxes. You might prefer to have the girls bring their own. The boxes need to be large enough to hold slips of paper about the size of business cards. Cover the boxes with fabric scraps, wallpaper or wrapping paper. Add ribbons, beads or craft jewels. Shells would also be pretty.

Cut pieces of paper about the size of calling cards. You may be able to find some labels the right size at an office supply store. Just trim away the part you don't need, but leave the backing on the labels to make them sturdy. The girls will write on the paper blessings that they find in God's Word. Then when they're having a discouraging day, they can look at the notes in the Blessing Box. Encourage the girls to pass blessings to one another and share favorite verses with each other. If they're having trouble thinking about what to write down, make some suggestions based on the promises of God.

Step 2: Bible Study Tips

Find out how well the girls have prepared the lesson in advance and adjust your class time accordingly. Begin your Bible study time by talking about positive and negative personality characteristics. Ask the girls:

- What kinds of things drive you nuts when other people do them?
- What kinds of things make you admire someone else?
- What do you think makes the difference between these two kinds of people?

Write these words on slips of paper and place them in a basket or paper lunch sack. Have the girls take a slip one at a time and talk about how the word describes a positive or negative characteristic in a person. Do as many as you have time for.

Sincere	Trustworthy	Dependable	Rushed
Impatient	Loving	Selfish	Loyal
Bragging	Forgiving		

Walk through the lesson pages together, pausing to look up verses and share reflections. As you come to the end of your time, focus on the concept that a person's character depends on what is in the person's heart. Use Digging for Seeds of Faith to talk about what God wants for our hearts.

• •

Treasures of the Heart ANSWERS

What kinds of heart troubles keep you from showing the treasure in your heart? Read the verses listed below. Then match each one to the "heart trouble" that it can help solve.

Philippians 4:13	For the discouraged heart, Christ gives strength.
1 Thessalonians 5:16	For the sad heart, God gives joy.
James 1:19–20	For the angry heart, God says watch your tongue.
John 14:1	For the worried heart, God says to trust Him.

How do your friends affect what is in your heart? Read each of these verses and then write down something that the verses teach you about choosing your friends.

1 Corinthians 15:33	Bad company corrupts character.
Proverbs 12:26	Caution in friendship; avoid the wicked.
Psalm 119:63	Be friends with those who know God.
Romans 12:9	Love is sincere.
1 Samuel 16:7	Look at the heart.
Proverbs 22:1	Good name means good reputation.

• •

Step 3: Manners Matter

The girls in your class are at an important age for developing friendships. Every parent knows that sometimes kids speak before they think or act impulsively. Use this time to talk about sharing what's really in our hearts with friends. We show what's in our hearts by the way we treat our friends. Discuss together what would be the right thing to do in each of these situations:

- Someone you don't really like invites you to a party and you say no. Later someone you do like invites you to the same party. Should you go?
- You've had a best friend since second grade and you spend a lot of time together. Now you have a new friend. How can you spend time with your new friend without hurting the feelings of your old friend?
- A friend gives you a gift that you don't really like. What do you say?
- Your friend has been borrowing lunch money a lot lately. She never pays you back. You're starting to get bugged. What should you do?
- Your two best friends are mad at each other. They both want you to take sides. What do you do?

Step 4: Wrapping Up

Have the girls get their Blessings Boxes. Invite them to share one blessing and read it aloud for the group. After each one, have the whole group respond, "The Lord is good to us." Pray together and close by singing "Blest the Pure in Heart." You'll find the music on pages 141.

Blest the pure in heart. They shall see your face
As they gaze upon You, captured by Your grace.
Father, You alone are the Holy One.
Stamp upon my heart, Lord, the image of Your Son.

What Am I Holding?

Step 1: Life Craft

You will need the following supplies to teach the girls how to care for their hands: bowls with soapy water (Use a fruity smelling shampoo instead of dish soap. It's less drying to the skin.), towels, nailpolish remover, cotton balls, nail files or clippers, and several pretty shades of nailpolish. As the girls arrive, pair each girl with a mentor who will give her a manicure—explaining each step as she goes. Remove all old polish first. Soak hands in bowls for a few minutes before rinsing and drying each hand. Using a nailfile or clippers, trim any broken or uneven nails. Apply one or two light coats of nail polish. If time allows, apply a nice hand cream after the polish is completely dry. If possible, send each girl home with a small bottle of hand lotion.

Step 2: Bible Study Tips

Find out how many of the girls have completed the study ahead of time. Adapt the depth of your discussion to how prepared the girls are and what you already know about their spiritual experience.

You'll need a small soft ball or a bean bag for this lesson. Gather the girls in a tight circle. Begin by giving the ball or bean bag to one of the girls. Their task is to find a way to pass the ball or bean bag all the way around the circle—without using their hands! If anyone uses her hands, she has to start over. When they've succeeded, talk about their experience.

- How did it feel to have someone take care of your hands?
- Give an example of how life would be different if you didn't have hands.

Walk through the lesson pages together, pausing to read the verses and share reflections. Be ready with some examples from your own life. You can enrich your discussion by looking up each of these passages together and talking about how Jesus used His hands.

- Matthew 8:1–3   Jesus heals a man with leprosy
  By reaching out with His hand, Jesus showed His willingness to serve. How do you use your hands to show that you're willing to do something?
- Matthew 8:14, 15   Jesus heals Peter's mother-in-law
  Jesus touched her hand with His hand. Why do you think holding someone's hand feels so comforting?
- Mark 5:35–42   Jesus heals Jairus's daughter
  Jesus took the girls' hand and also spoke to her. Share some experiences when touch and words together helped someone.
- John 9:1–11   Jesus heals a blind man
  Jesus wasn't afraid to get His hands dirty to do God's work. Share some examples when it may be messy to serve other people.

The lesson asked the girls to share some ways to show kindness using their hands. Find out what ideas they came up with. Brainstorm some more ways together. Encourage the girls to be very specific and give realistic examples from their own lives.

As you come to the end of the lesson, focus on the fact that we use our hands dozens—even hundreds—of different ways every day. Many times we don't even think about what we're doing with our hands; they seem to have a mind of their own! God made every part of our bodies in a marvelous way. He wants us to use our hands to bring honor and glory to Him.

. . . .

Hands to Help and Hands to Hold A N s w e r s

There are no right or wrong answers for the questions in this week's Digging for Seeds of Faith. The questions challenge the girls to think of specific examples of how they can use their hands to serve God. Encourage the girls to share the examples they've thought of. If you have time, brainstorm together for more examples and challenge the girls to choose one idea to follow through on this week.

. . . .

Step 3: Manners Matter   Plan Wind-Up + iLWK Kit

Use some nice dishes and invite the girls to set the table together. Depending on the size of your group, you may want to set several tables. Make sure they know where to place the silverware, glasses and napkins for a proper table setting. Use a simple floral arrangement and candles for a centerpiece. Talk about how what they do with their hands in setting a pretty table helps guests feel welcome and valued. If you'd like, you could serve some simple refreshments and let the girls enjoy the fruit of their labor at the table.

Step 4: Wrapping Up

Close by praying together and thanking God for hands. Sing a song about lifting our hands and hearts to God.

Where Am I Going?

Step 1: Life Craft

Gather these supplies: one small wide-mouthed glass jar for each girl (small jelly or olive jars work), tempera paint and brushes, beads and other trim, tacky glue, coarse salt such as sea salt or rock salt (enough to half-fill each jar), ribbon with paper tag and one votive candle for each jar. Optional: One or your mentors may wish to write out the verses on the tags in pretty calligraphy before class.

As the girls arrive, encourage them to select a jar to decorate. The jars do not need to be exactly the same in size or shape. The girls may paint designs on the jars and attach trim with glue. Fill each jar half full with coarse salt and place a candle securely in the center. Have the girls write Matthew 5:13 ("You are the salt of the earth") on one side of the tag and Matthew 5:16 ("Let your light so shine before men") on the other side before tying the ribbon around the mouth of the jar. The girls now have a wonderful reminder to be salt and light wherever they go.

Step 2: Bible Study Tips

Gather a box or duffel bag full of different kinds of shoes that the girls will recognize, such as tennis shoes, specialty sports shoes, sandals, slippers, dress shoes, and high heels. Pass the bag around the group and ask girls to reach in and pull out a shoe. Then have the girl with a shoe talk about what occasions that shoe is appropriate for. Then ask:

- Why does it matter what we put on our feet for different situations?
- Why are feet important to the body?

Walk through the lesson pages together, pausing to read the verses and share reflections. You can enrich your discussion with these ideas:

- Invite the girls to share athletic experiences of their own. What kept them going when they felt like giving up? What does winning feel like?

- Talk more in depth about how important training is to an athlete. Then bring out the parts of the lesson that talk about training for the race of life.
- Talk about why people admire champion athletes. Use this discussion as a transition into talking about people who are examples to us for running the race of life.

As you come to the end of the lesson, focus on the importance of walking a consistent Christian life in front of other people, including friends and family who see us every day. Digging for Seeds of Faith will help you with this discussion. Invite the girls to share examples of people they admire for consistent faith and wise action.

· ·

Run With God A N S W E R S

Psalm 119:32	**Run in the path of God's commands.**
Isaiah 30:21	**Listen to God's voice and follow it.**
Proverbs 3:5-6	**Trust God, and not just yourself.**
Hebrews 12:1	**Run with perseverance.**
Isaiah 40:31	**Hope in the Lord and you will not become weary.**
Psalm 119:105	**Let God's Word show you where to go.**
Proverbs 4:11, 12	**Let God guide you in the right path.**
Psalm 121:3	**Depend on God to keep you from slipping.**

· ·

Step 3: Manners Matter

Put feet on God's love! Learning to serve others at a young age will help your girls form the habit of service. Choose a service project that you can do together. This might be baking for the shut-ins from your church congregation, working with younger children in a planned event, or doing chores or errands for someone who needs a little extra help.

An important part of service is having a gracious, humble spirit. As you plan your project, take time to help the girls prepare to show the heart of a servant. Practice things they could say that would be appropriate to the setting of your project. Review some of the introductions, conversation starters and manners that you've learned in previous sessions. Talk about how they apply to the project.

Step 4: Wrapping Up

Take a few minutes to pray for the girls in your group. Invite mentors to put their hands on the heads and shoulders of the girls as you pray for them individually. You might also want to give the girls an opportunity to pray for each other.

Close your last class together by singing the song below. You'll find the music on page 142.

> I pray for you, my child, a life that's filled with laughter;
> That you will know the joy of Christ within your soul.
> And when temptations come, I pray that you will trust Him,
> Knowing He holds all things in His control.
> I pray for you, my child, that you will know the Father,
> And trust in Jesus Christ, His one and only Son,
> And may the Holy Spirit's favor rest upon you
> Until your race for Him on earth is done.

BETTY HUIZENGA, © 1999

. . . .

Mentor's Covenant

1. I covenant that I have accepted Jesus Christ as my Lord and Savior, and seek to honor him in my life.

2. I will seek to be a servant of the Lord in the program of *Appleseeds*.

3. I will prepare the lessons ahead of time, those I teach and all other lessons as well.

4. I will faithfully pray for the *Appleseeds* program and for each participant in the class.

5. I will make every effort to befriend each person in the class and make myself available to them as needed.

6. I will attend all classes, Lord willing. If I am unable to attend a class, I will clear my absence with other leaders.

       Signature_____

       Date_____

. . . .

Participant's Covenant

1. I will be a faithful participant in the *Appleseeds* class, not missing more than one lesson, Lord willing.

2. I will pray for the ministry of *Appleseeds* and for my leaders.

3. I will prepare each lesson in advance, asking the Lord to give me wisdom and insight, and a heart open to obey what He shows me through the lesson and class.

       Signature_____

       Date_____

. . . .

THE SONGS

I SUBMIT, O FATHER

Betty Huizenga

LOVING YOUR CHILDREN

BLEST THE PURE IN HEART

A MOTHER'S PRAYER

Betty Huizenga

renewing the heart®

Truth and Grace for Daily Living

Welcome to a Special Place Just for Women

We hope you've enjoyed this book.
Renewing the Heart, a ministry of Focus on the Family,
is dedicated to equipping and encouraging women in all facets of their
lives. Through our weekly call-in radio program, our Web site, and a
variety of other outreaches, Renewing the Heart is a place to find
answers, gain support, and, most of all, know you're among friends.

How to Reach Us

For more information and additional resources, visit our Web site at
www.renewingtheheart.com. Here, you'll find articles, devotions, and
broadcast information on our weekly call-in radio program,
"Renewing the Heart," hosted by Janet Parshall.

To request any of these resources, call Focus on the Family at
800-A-FAMILY (800-232-6459). In Canada, call 800-661-9800.

You may also write us at:
Focus on the Family, Colorado Springs, CO 80995

In Canada, write to: Focus on the Family,
P.O. Box 9800, Stn. Terminal, Vancouver, B.C. V6B 4G3

To learn more about Focus on the Family or to find out if we have an
associate office in your country, please visit www.family.org.

We'd love to hear from you!

About the Author

Betty Huizenga began the *Apples of Gold* seminars in her home many years ago, and now other women are duplicating the seminars around the country. After she and her husband retired, Betty felt the Lord calling her to minister to younger women. She and her husband now divide their time between Michigan and Florida.

Apples of Gold

The life-changing principles of Betty's seminars come to life in book form, offering women an encouraging plan for developing kindness, purity, hospitality, and love for their children and husband. ISBN: 978-0-7814-3352-5

Gifts of Gold

A book that both encourages and equips mentors, this important tool answers questions about why mentoring is so vital to today's women and calls every woman to embrace her heritage as a Christian while responding to the call of Titus 2 to teach the younger women.
ISBN: 978-0-7814-3809-4

LaVergne, TN USA
30 September 2010
198976LV00004BA/4/P